Wrestling with the Devil

Also by Ngũgĩ wa Thiong'o

Novels (English)

The River Between

Weep Not, Child

A Grain of Wheat

Petals of Blood

Devil on the Cross

Matigari

Wizard of the Crow

Short Stories (English)

Secret Lives

Novels (Gĩkũyũ)

Caitani Mũtharabainĩ

Matigari ma Njirũngi

Mũrogi wa Kagogo

Plays (English)

The Black Hermit

This Time Tomorrow

The Trial of Dedan Kĩmathi (with Micere Mugo)

I Will Marry When I Want (with Ngũgĩ wa Mĩriĩ)

Plays (Gĩkũyũ)

Ngaahika Ndeenda (with Ngũgĩ wa Mĩriĩ)

Maitũ Njugĩra

Essays (English)

Homecoming

Moving the Center

Penpoints, Gunpoints, and Dreams

Decolonizing the Mind

Something Torn and New (also issued under the
title *Re-Membering Africa*)

Globalectics: Theory and Politics of Knowing

In the Name of the Mother

Secure the Base: Making Africa Visible in the Globe

Memoirs (English)

Dreams in a Time of War

In the House of the Interpreter

Birth of a Dream Weaver

Children's Books (English)

Njamba Nene and the Flying Bus

Njamba Nene's Pistol

Children's Books (Gĩkũyũ)

Njamba Nene na Mbathi ĩ Mathagu

Bathitora ya Njamba Nene

Rwĩmbo rwa Njũkĩ

Allegory (Gĩkũyũ)

Nyoni Nyonia Nyone

Wrestling with the Devil

A PRISON MEMOIR

Ngũgĩ wa Thiong'o

THE NEW PRESS

NEW YORK
LONDON

Requests for permission to reproduce selections from this book should be mailed to:
Permissions Department, The New Press, 120 Wall Street, 31st floor, New York, NY
10005.

Photographs and sculptures on pages 2 and 241 by Pitika Ntuli

Published in the United States by The New Press, New York, 2018
Distributed by Two Rivers Distribution

ISBN 978-1-62097-333-2 (hc)
ISBN 978-1-62097-334-9 (e-book)
CIP is available

The New Press publishes books that promote and enrich public discussion and
understanding of the issues vital to our democracy and to a more equitable world.
These books are made possible by the enthusiasm of our readers; the support of a
committed group of donors, large and small; the collaboration of our many partners
in the independent media and the not-for-profit sector; booksellers, who often hand-
sell New Press books; librarians; and above all by our authors.

www.thenewpress.com

Book design and composition by Bookbright Media
This book was set in Garamond Premier Pro

Printed in the United States of America

10 9 8 7 6 5 4 3 2 1

To all writers in prisons
and for a world without
prisons and detention camps

O you with bloodshot eyes and bloody hands,
Night is short-lived,
The detention room lasts not forever,
Nor yet the links of chains.

> —*Mahmoud Darwish, from "About a Man," in*
> The Music of Human Flesh, *translated by Denys*
> *Johnson-Davies*

Contents

Note to this Edition

This book is developed from *Detained: A Writer's Prison Diary*, originally published in 1982, when Kenya was under the reign of terror of a one-person, one-party state, not the case today, as I edit this, in 2017. Considerably shorter and leaner because shorn of many dated historical references and documents, it has allowed focus on the drama of the writing of a novel, *Devil on the Cross*, in prison. I have also added details on the final fate of the novel, which I had left out in the earlier edition.

I offer this re-edited version of my experience of survival in a maximum-security prison as a testimony to the magic of imagination. The power of imagination to help humans break free of confinement is truly the story of all art.

Wrestling with the Devil

DETENTION ORDER

THE PUBLIC SECURITY DETAINED AND RESTRICTED PERSONS (REGULATIONS 1966)

DETENTION ORDER

In exercise of the powers conferred by regulation 6, (1) of the Public Security (Detained and Restricted Persons) Regulations 1966, the Minister for Home Affairs, being satisfied that it is necessary for the preservation of public security to exercise control, beyond that afforded by a restriction order, over

NGŨGĨ WA THIONG'O

(hereinafter referred to as the detained person), HEREBY ORDERS that the person shall be detained.

. . .

Date this 29th December 1977

(D. T. Arap Moi),

MINISTER FOR HOME AFFAIRS

Solitary Confinement

1

Free Thoughts on Toilet Paper

1

It is past midnight, December 12, 1978. Unable to face the prick-
ly bristles of three see-through blankets on a mattress whose
sisal stuffing has folded into numerous lumps hard as stones, I
am at the desk, under the full electric glare of a hundred-watt
naked bulb, scribbling words on toilet paper. I can hear the
bootsteps of the night guard, going up and down the passageway between the two rows of cells, which face each other.

Mine is cell 16 in a prison block enclosing eighteen other
political prisoners. Here I have no name. I am just a number
in a file: K6,77. A tiny iron frame against one wall serves as a
bed. A tiny board against another wall serves as a desk. These
fill up the minute cell.

One end of the passageway is a cul-de-sac of two latrines,
a washroom with only one sink and a shower room for four.
These are all open: no doors. At the other end, next to my
cell, the passageway opens into a tiny exercise yard whose
major features are one aluminum rubbish bin and a decrepit
tenniquoit-*cum*-volleyball net hanging from two iron poles.

There is a door of iron bars at this opening—between the exercise yard and the block of cells—and it is always shut and locked at night. The block of cells and the yard are enclosed by four double stone walls so high that they completely cut off the skyline of trees and buildings, which might otherwise give us a glimpse of the world of active life.

This is Kamĩtĩ Maximum Security Prison, one of the largest in Africa. It is situated near three towns—Rũirũ, Kĩambu, and Nairobi—and literally next door to Kenyatta University College, but we could as easily be on Mars. We are completely quarantined from everything and everybody, including convicted prisoners in all the other blocks, except for a highly drilled select squad of prison guards and their commanding officers.

Maximum security: the idea used to fill me with terror whenever I met it in fiction, Dickens mostly, and I have always associated it with England and Englishmen; it conjured up images of hordes of dangerous killers à la Magwitch of *Great Expectations*, always ready to escape through thick forests and marshes, to unleash yet more havoc and terror on an otherwise stable, peaceful, and God-fearing community of property owners that sees itself as the whole society. It also conjures images of Robben Island political prisoners, Mandela among them, breaking rocks for no purpose other than breaking them. A year as an inmate in Kamĩtĩ has taught me what should have been obvious: that the prison system is a repressive weapon in the hands of a ruling minority to ensure maximum security for its class dictatorship over the rest of the population, and it is not a monopoly exclusive to England and South Africa.

The menacing bootsteps come nearer. I know that the prowling guard cannot enter my cell—it is always double-locked and the keys, in turn, locked inside a box, which promptly at five o'clock is taken away by the corporal on duty to a safe somewhere outside the double walls—but of course he can look into the cell through a small iron-barred rectangular window in the upper half of the door. The barred window is built so as to contain only the face.

The bootsteps stop. I don't have to look to the door to know that the guard is watching me. I can feel it in my bones. It is an instinct that one develops in prison, the cunning instinct of the hunted. I take my time, and eventually turn my eyes to the door. The face of the guard fills the whole window: I know nothing so menacingly sinister in its silent stillness as that trunkless face glaring at one through the iron bars of a prison cell.

"Professor, . . . why are you not in bed?" the voice redeems the face. "What are you doing?"

Relief! I fall back on the current witticism in the detention block.

"I am writing to Jomo Kenyatta in his capacity as an ex–political prisoner."

"His case was different," the guard argues.

"How?"

"His was a colonial affair."

"And this, a neocolonial affair? What's the difference?"

"A colonial affair . . . now we are independent—that's the difference," he says.

"A colonial affair in an independent country, eh? The British jailed an innocent Kenyatta. Thus Kenyatta learned to jail innocent Kenyans. Is that the difference?"

He laughs. Then he repeats it.

"The British jailed Kenyatta. Kenyatta jails Kenyans." He laughs again, adding, "Take it any way you like, . . . but write a good petition . . . you might get a hearing this time. . . . Your star shines bright in the sky . . . ex–political prisoner." He chuckles to himself. "Does 'ex-' mean the same thing as 'late'—*hayati*?"

"What do you mean?"

"Can I say the late political prisoner instead of the ex–political prisoner?"

The tone tells me that he knows the difference and that he is trying to communicate something. But tonight I feel a little impatient.

"You know I no longer teach English," I say to him.

"You never can tell the language of the stars," he persists. "Once a teacher, always a teacher," he says, and goes away laughing.

In his prison notes, *The Man Died*, Wole Soyinka aptly comments that "no matter how cunning a prisoner, the humanitarian act of courage among his gaolers plays a key role in his survival."

This guard is a good illustration of the truth of that observation. He is the one who in March told me about the formation of the London-based Ngũgĩ Defence Committee and the subsequent picketing of the Kenyan Embassy on March 3, 1978. He enjoys talking in riddles and communicating in a roundabout way. It's a way of protecting himself, of course, but he enjoys seeing a prisoner grope for the hidden meanings, if any. Tonight, his laughter sounds more direct and sympathetic, or perhaps it is another kind of riddle to be taken any way I like.

Two guards walk the passageway in turns. One sleeps, the other is awake. At one o'clock they change places. They too cannot get out because the door between the passageway and the exercise yard is locked and the keys taken away. Night warders are themselves prisoners guarding other prisoners. Only they are paid for it and their captivity is self-inflicted or else imposed by lack of alternative means of life. One very young guard—a Standard Seven[1] dropout—tells me that his ambition is to be a fighter pilot! Another, a grandfather, tells me his ambition once was to become a musician.

To hell with the guards! Away with intruding thoughts! Tonight I don't want to think about guards and prisoners, colonial or neocolonial affairs. I am totally engrossed in Waringa, the fictional heroine of the novel I have been writing on toilet paper for the last ten months or so![2]

Toilet paper: when in the 1960s I first read in Kwame Nkrumah's autobiography, *Ghana*, that in his cell at James Fort Prison he used to hoard toilet paper to write on, I thought it was romantic and a little unreal despite the photographic evidence reproduced in the book. Writing on toilet paper?

Now I know: paper, any paper, is about the most precious article for a political prisoner, more so for one, like me, who was imprisoned without trial for his writing. For the urge to write . . .

Picking the jagged bits embedded in my mind,
Partly to wrench some ease for my own mind,
And partly that some world sometime may know

. . . is almost irresistible to a political prisoner.

{ Ndi }[1]

Macaria akĩrũmarũmia Waringa guoko. Ngoro-inĩ ndaathirĩĩtwo nĩ kĩũũndũ gĩa kwĩiigua ta aarĩ o kĩrooto-inĩ, akaigua ta hiihi aangĩgurumũka akore andũ acio moombũkĩĩte. No aksigua Waringa naake aamũrũ marũmia. Macaria akĩmenya atĩ o na aakorwo we nĩ kĩrooto-inĩ aarĩ, o naake Waringa aarĩ o kuo kĩrooto-inĩ. Magĩikara ũguo manyiitanĩĩte mooko, o mũũndũ na meeciiria

At Kamītī, virtually all the political prisoners are writing or composing something, on toilet paper, mostly. Now the same good old toilet paper—which had served Kwame Nkrumah in James Fort Prison, Dennis Brutus on Robben Island, Abdilatif Abdalla in G Block, Kamītī, and countless other persons with similar urges—has enabled me to defy daily the intended detention and imprisonment of my mind.

> A flicker, pulse, mere vital hint
> which speaks of the stubborn will
> the grim assertion of some sense of worth
> in the teeth of the wind
> on a stony beach, or among rocks
> where the brute hammers fall unceasingly
> on the mind.

I now know what Brutus meant. Writing this novel has been a daily, almost hourly, assertion of my will to remain human and free despite the state's program of animal degradation of political prisoners.

Privacy, for instance. I mean its brutal invasion. A warder trails me waking and sleeping for twenty-four hours. It is unnerving, truly unnerving, to find a guard watching me shit and urinate into a children's chamber pot in my cell, or to find him standing by the entrance to the toilet to watch me do the same exercise. The electric light is on all night long. To induce sleep, I tie a towel over my eyes. This ends up straining them, so that after a month they start smarting and watering. But even more painful is to wake up in the middle of the night, from a dreamless slumber or one softened by sweet illusion or riddled with nightmares, to find two bodiless eyes fixed on me through the iron bars.

Or monotony: the human mind revolts against endless sameness. In ordinary social life, even the closest-knit family hardly ever spends a whole day together on the same compound in meaningless circles. Man, woman, and child go about their different activities in different places and meet only in the evening to recount their different experiences. Experiments done on animals show that when they are confined to a small space and subjected to the same routine they end up tearing each other apart. Now the Kenyatta government was doing the same experiment on human beings.

At Kamĩtĩ, we daily see the same faces in the same white prison uniforms we call *kũngũrũ*; for food, we are on corn and beans in the morning, at noon, and at three o'clock. Our life here goes through the same motions, day in day out, in a confined space of reliefless dust and gray stones. The two most dominant colors in the detention block are white and gray, and I am convinced these are the colors of death.

The officials cannot have been ignorant of the possible results of these experiments in mental torment: Valium is the most frequently prescribed drug. The doctor expects a political prisoner to be mad or depressed unless proved otherwise.

There is a history to it. I was told a harrowing story of one political prisoner in this very block but before my time who had had a mental breakdown. The authorities watched him go down the drain, till he was reduced to eating his own feces. Yet the regime kept him in that condition for two years.

A week after my incarceration, Wasonga Sijeyo, who has been in that block for nine years but has managed to keep a razor-sharp mind and a heart of steel, eluded the vigilant eyes of the warder then guarding me, and within seconds he told me words that I have come to treasure:

"It may sound a strange thing to say to you, but in a sense I am glad they brought you here. The other day—in fact a week or so before you came—we were saying that it would be a good thing for Kenya if more intellectuals were imprisoned. First, it would wake most of them from their illusions. And some of them might outlive jail to tell the world. The thing is . . . just watch your mind. . . . Don't let them break you and you'll be all right even if they keep you for life, . . . but you must try . . . you have to, for us, for the ones you left behind."

Besides being an insurrection of a detained intellect, the writing of this novel has been one way of keeping my mind and heart together.

2

I had given myself a difficult task. I would write in Gĩkũyũ, a language that did not yet have a modern novel, as a challenge to myself, a way of affirming my faith in the possibilities of the languages of all the different Kenyan nationalities, languages whose growth as vehicles for people's struggles and development had been actively suppressed by the British colonial regime (1895–1963) and now its postcolonial successor. I had resolved not to make any concessions to the language. I would not avoid any subject—science, technology, philosophy, religion, music, political economy—provided it logically arose out of the development of the novel's theme, character, plot, story, and world view. Furthermore, I would use everything I had ever learned about the craft of fiction—allegory, parable, satire, narrative, description, reminiscence, flashback, interior monologue, stream of consciousness, dialogue, drama—provided it came naturally in the development of character, theme, and story. Content—not language and technique—would determine the eventual form of the novel.

Easier said than done: where was I to get the inspiration? Writers need people around them. They thrive on live struggles of active life. Contrary to popular mythology, a novel is not the sole product of the imaginative feats of a single individual but the work of many hands and tongues. Writers just take down notes dictated to them by life among the people, which they then arrange in this or that form. In writing a novel, I love to hear the voices of people working the land, forging metal in a factory, telling anecdotes in a crowded *matatu* (public minibus), gyrating their hips in a crowded bar before a jukebox or a live band—people playing the games of love and hate and fear and glory in their struggle to live. I need to look at different people's faces, their gestures, their gait, their clothes, and to hear the variegated modulations of their voices in different moods. I need the vibrant voices of beautiful women: their touches, their sighs, their tears, their laughter. I like the presence of children prancing about, fighting, laughing, crying. I need life to write about life.

But it is also true that nobody writes under one's chosen conditions with one's chosen material. Writers can only seize the time to select from material handed to them by history and by whomever and whatever is around them. So my case now: I had not chosen prison; I was forced into it, but now that I'm there, I will try to turn the double-walled enclosure into a special school where, like Shakespeare's *Richard II*, I will study how I might compare:

> This prison where I live unto the world, ...
> My brain I'll prove the female to my soul,
> My soul the father; and history and these two beget
> A generation of still-breeding thoughts,
> And these same thoughts people this little world,
> In humours like the people of this world,
> For no thought is contented.

In this literary target, I am lucky to have for teachers the other political prisoners and a few guards, who are cooperative and very generous in sharing their different mines of information and experience. But mostly I pick a lot from ordinary meandering conversations, when in groups we talk of women of various careers—barmaids, secretaries, teachers, and engineers—as well as different aspects of social life and bourgeois rivalry in Nairobi. Women may be absent from the block, but they sure dominate regular talk among us, mostly as absent actors in titillating narratives of strange encounters, rejections, broken hearts, and conquests.

Not only discussions, direct inquiries, and riveting dramas of the heart, but also whispers of happenings outside the walls often provide me with material that I weave into the fabric of the novel. In fact, hints of the main theme and story line emerged when I learned of two members of parliament serving sentences after being convicted of coffee theft. Tidbits about the South African heart surgeon Christiaan Barnard's[3] visit and his racist pro-apartheid views, promulgated on public platforms his Kenyan hosts had generously provided him, have prompted the philosophical discussion in a *matatu* about "life to come" and the problem of rival claims to the same heart on the day of resurrection. These bits of news also have led to my satirical depiction of one robber character who longs for a world in which the wealthy few gain immortality by buying spare organs, leaving death as the sole prerogative of the poor.

In the daytime, I take hasty notes on empty spaces of the Bible, one of the books freely allowed in the cells. I scribble notes on the bare walls of my cell, and in the evening try to put it all together on toilet paper.

Sometimes the bug of literary boredom and despair bites me, and I experience those painful moments when writers begin to doubt the value of what they are scribbling or the possibility of ever completing the task in hand—those moments when writers restrain themselves with difficulty from setting the thing on fire, or tearing it into pieces, or abandoning it all to dust and cobwebs. These moments—the writer's block—are worse in prison because here, in this desolate place, there are no distractions to massage the tired imagination: a glass of beer, a sound of music, or a long walk in sun and wind or under a calm starry sky.

But at those very moments, I remind myself that the state has sent me here for my brain to melt into a rotten mess, and suddenly I feel the call to a spiritual battle against its bestial purposes. Time and again, the defiance charges me with new energy and determination: I must cheat them out of that last laugh; I must let my imagination loose over the kind of society that those in this class, in nakedly treacherous alliance with imperialism, are building in our country, in cynical disregard of the wishes of many millions of Kenyans.

Because women are the most exploited and oppressed of all working people, I would create a picture of a strong, determined woman with a will to resist and struggle against her present conditions. Had I not seen glimpses of this type in real life among the women of Kamĩrĩthũ Community Education and Cultural Centre, with whom I worked to produce the play *Ngaahika Ndeenda*?[4] Isn't Kenyan history replete with this type of woman?—Me Katilili wa Menza,[5] Muraa wa Ngiti,[6] Mary Mũthoni Nyanjirũ,[7] and the women soldiers of the Kenya Land and Freedom Army? Warĩnga will be the fictional reflection of the spirit of women's resistance and resilience in Kenyan history.

Warĩnga ngatha ya wĩra, Warĩnga heroine of toil . . . there she walks haughtily carrying her freedom in her own hands. . . .

Now I am on the last chapter. I have given myself December 25, 1978, as the deadline. The date has a special significance for me. In February or early March, I had told the other political prisoners that we would all "eat Christmas" at home. I even invited them to a Christmas *nyama choma* party at my home in Gĩtogothi, Bibirioni, Limuru. Like so many other prison wagers related to dreams of eventual liberty, the goat-meat roasting party at Christmas was announced half in jest, but I secretly believed in it and inwardly clung to the date, though becoming less and less openly assertive about it as days and nights rolled away. Now only twelve days remain. Twelve days to eat Christmas at home. Twelve days to meet my self-imposed literary deadline!

But tonight something else, an impulse, a voice, is urging me to run this last lap faster. The voice is not all that secret. Maybe it is born of the feverish expectation of early release, which has been building up in the block for the last four months, though now nobody is sure of its ifs and whens. Maybe it is also born of a writer's usual excitement at seeing the light at the end of a long, hazardous tunnel. Maybe it's a combination of both, but whatever its source, the voice remains insistent.

The heart is willing. The hand that has been scribbling non-stop from about seven o'clock is weak. But the voice is relentless: Write on!

I rise to stretch my legs. I walk to the iron-barred rectangular window and peer into the passageway. The two guards are playing checkers, but they are murmuring more than they are playing. I ask the same guard about the time.

"Half-past twelve," he says, and then adds, "Why do you want to know the time, Professor?"

"I wanted to know if my star is still shining in the sky," I answer.

"You better have some sleep. You might need it."

No. I don't feel like any sleep tonight. I go back to the desk to resume the race to the literary tape, now only a couple of paragraphs away. Free thoughts on toilet paper!

3

In front of me is a photograph of my daughter Njoki, meaning "she who comes back from the other world"; or Aiyerubo, meaning "she who defies heaven and hell"; or Wamũingĩ, meaning "she who belongs to the people." Later, when I am out of Kamĩtĩ, I will see her and hold her in my arms and learn that she was named Wamũingĩ by the peasant women of Limuru, Aiyerubo by Wole Soyinka and the Writers of African Peoples in Nigeria, but just now she is only a name and a photograph sent through the mail.

Njoki was born on May 15, 1978, five months after my abduction. When her photograph arrived in Kamĩtĩ, sometime after that defiant break into life, Thairũ wa Mũthĩga, a fellow inmate, nicknamed her Kaana ka Bothita, Post-Office Baby.

In saying that the post office has brought us luck, Thairũ spoke a truth I felt more than thought. Njoki is a message from the world. A message of hope. A message that, somewhere, outside these gray walls of death, people were waiting for me, thinking about me, perhaps even fighting for my release with whatever weapons they had. A protest, a hastily muttered prayer from the lips of a peasant, a groan, a sigh, wishes of helpless children: today such gestures and wishes may not be horses on which seekers of freedom may ride to liberty, but I embrace them as offerings of a much needed moral solidarity with us and with the issues for which we have been jailed. One day the organized power and united will of millions will transform these moral wishes into people's chariots of actual freedom from ruthless exploitation and naked oppression, but just now merely sensing them through Njoki's photograph is a daily source of joyful strength.

The act of imprisoning democrats, progressive intellectuals, and militant workers reveals many things. It is first an admission by the authorities that they know they have been *seen*. By signing the detention orders, they acknowledge that the people have seen through their official lies labeled as a new philosophy, their pretensions wrapped in three-piece suits and gold chains, their propaganda packaged as religious truth, their plastic smiles ordered from abroad, their nationally televised charitable handouts and breast-beatings before the high altar, their high-sounding phrases and ready-to-shed tears at the sight of naked children fighting cats and dogs for a trash heap, that all have seen these performances of benign benevolence for what they truly are: a calculated sugarcoating of the immoral sale and mortgage of a whole country, its people and resources, to Euro-American and Japanese capital[8] for a few million dollars in Swiss banks and a few token shares in foreign companies.

Their vaunted morality is nothing more than the elevation of begging and charity into desirable moral ideals. There is a newfound dignity in begging. Charity, for them, is twice-blessed; it deflates the self-esteem of the recipients and their will to fight, and it inflates the self-image of the giver.

Recourse to imprisonment, with or without a trial, is above all an admission by the ruling minority that people have started to organize to oppose the plunder of the national wealth and heritage. It fears that the people might rise in arms, and therefore acts to forestall such an uprising, real or imaginary.

Thus detention and imprisonment more immediately mean the physical removal of progressive intellectuals from the people's organized struggles. Ideally, the authorities would like to put the whole community of struggling millions behind bars, as the British colonial authorities once tried to do with Kenyan people during the State of Emergency,[9] but this would mean incarcerating labor, the true source of national wealth. What then would be left to loot? So the authorities do the simpler thing: pick one or two individuals from among the people and then loudly claim that all sins lie at the feet of these "power hungry," "misguided," and "ambitious" agitators.

Any awakening of a people to their historic mission of liberating themselves from oppression is always denounced by the oppressor with the religious rhetoric of a wronged, self-righteous god. Suddenly, these "agitators" become devils whose removal from society is portrayed as a divine mission. Chain the devils! The people are otherwise innocent, simple, peace-loving, obedient, law-abiding, and cannot conceivably harbor any desire to change this best of all possible worlds. It is partly self-deception, but also an attempted deception of millions.

Political detention and imprisonment, besides their punitive aspects, serve as exemplary ritual symbolism. If the state can break such progressive nationalists, if they can make them come out of prison crying, "I am sorry for all my sins," such an unprincipled about-face would confirm the wisdom of the ruling clique in its division of the populace into the passive innocent millions and the disgruntled subversive few. The "confession" and its expected corollary, "Father, forgive us our sins," become a cleansing ritual for all the past and current repression. For a few tidbits, directorship of this or that statutory body, the privilege of running for parliament on the regime's party ticket, such an ex–political prisoner might even happily play the role of a conscientious messenger sent back to earth from purgatory by a father figure more benevolent than Lazarus's Abraham, "that he may testify unto them, lest they also come into this place of torment." The forgiving father sits back to enjoy international applause for his manifold munificence and compassion.

Even when they find that such a political prisoner is not in a position to play the role of an active preacher against the futility of struggle (they may have damaged him or her beyond any exploitable repair), they can still publicize this picture of a human wreck as a warning to all future agitators: they couldn't stand it; do you think you are made of sterner steel? The former hardcore patriot or matriot is physically, intellectually, and spiritually broken, and by a weird symbolic extension, so is the whole struggling populace. All is well in imperialist heaven, for now there is peace on neocolonial earth, policed by a tough no-nonsense comprador[10] ruling class that knows how to deal with subversive elements.

The fact is that imprisonment without trial is not only a punitive act of physical and mental torture of a few individuals; it is also a calculated act of psychological terror against the struggling millions. The aim is a psychological siege of the whole nation. That is why the process from the time of arrest to the time of release is deliberately invested with mystifying ritualism. My arrest, for instance.

4

They came for me at midnight. It was December 30, 1977, at Gĩtogothi, Bibirioni, Limuru. Two Land Rovers with police officers armed with machine guns, rifles, and pistols drove into the yard. A sedan flashing red and blue on its roof remained at the main gate, very much like the biblical sword of fire policing the ejection of Adam and Eve from the Garden of Eden by

God, who didn't want humans to eat from the tree of knowledge. The stability of Adamic Eden depended on its residents remaining ignorant about their condition. Behind the sedan were others that, as I later came to learn, carried some local administrative officials and a corps of informers. The latter remained lurking in the shadows for fear that, even at such a dark hour, some peasants around might recognize them and denounce them to the people.

Armed members of the Intelligence, then known as the Special Branch, who swarmed my study amid an awe-inspiring silence, were additionally guarded by uniformed police officers carrying long-range rifles. Their grim, determined faces lit up only a little whenever they pounced on any book or pamphlet bearing the names of Marx, Engels, or Lenin. I tried to lift the weight of silence in the room by remarking that if Lenin, Marx, or Engels were all they were after, I could save them much time and energy by showing them the shelves where these dangerous three were hiding. The leader of the book-raiding squad was not amused. He growled at me, so I took his "advice" and let them do their work without verbal interruptions.

I kept on darting my eyes from one raider to the other in case they planted something illegal, like banned pamphlets, so as then to claim they found them hidden among my other books. But I was alone and they were many, all over the study. I soon realized the futility of my vigilance, like the persona in a poem who warns the reader that:

It's no use
Your hiding deep in the dark well of your house
Hiding your words

Burning your books
It's no use.

They'll come to find you
In lorries, piled high with leaflets,
With letters no one ever wrote to you
They'll fill your passport with stamps
From countries where you have never been

They'll drag you away
Like some dead dog
And that night you'll find out all about torture
In the dark room
Where all the foul odours of the world are bred
It's no use
Your hiding
From the fight, my friend[11]

Nevertheless, in helpless silence, my eyes never strayed from the raiders' activities. To the list of works of the Dangerous Three, they now added Kim Chi Ha's *Cry of the People*, and any book whose title contained the words "scientific socialism."

And then they saw a pile of copies of *Ngaahika Ndeenda*. They crowded around it, each taking a copy, flipping through it, and then added the copies to the loot. They had arrested the playscript. It seemed they had accomplished their mission.

The conversation in my living room went something like this:

NGŨGĨ: Gentlemen, can I request that we sit down and record all the books and pamphlets you have taken?

POLICE: We shall do all that at the police station.

NGŨGĨ: Tell me quite frankly: Am I under arrest?

POLICE: Oh, no.

NGŨGĨ: In that case, I'll provide you with a table, pen, and paper, and we can record everything before it leaves the house.

POLICE: We shall do it at the station, and you are coming with us.

NGŨGĨ: What for?

POLICE: To answer a few questions.

NGŨGĨ: Am I under arrest?

POLICE : No.

NGŨGĨ: In that case, can't the questions wait until morning?

POLICE : No.

NGŨGĨ: Can you please give me a minute with my wife to sort out one thing or two?

POLICE : It is not necessary. We promise that you'll be back in the morning. Just a few questions.

NGŨGĨ: Can you tell me where you are taking me so that my wife here can know?

POLICE: Tigoni.[12]

This was an abduction. Still, I couldn't help musing over the fact that the police squadron was armed to the teeth to abduct a writer whose only acts of violent resistance were safely between the hard and soft covers of books.

5

Tigoni was the local police station, about six miles away. I was pushed into an empty room with bare walls where I was guarded by only one member of the abducting team. Now he smiled rather slyly and he asked me, "How come that as soon as we knocked at the door, you were already up and fully dressed?"

I had neither the time nor the necessary energy to tell him that I had had a premonition, that I had just returned home from Nairobi after saying a rather elaborate farewell to my drinking buddies at the Impala Hotel, that I had even firmly and repeatedly refused a beer, that I had driven from Impala Hotel, Nairobi, to Limuru at a snail's pace, literally no more than twenty-five miles per hour the whole way, that on arrival home, instead of putting on my pajamas and slipping into bed beside Nyambura, I just lay on the cover fully clad, staring at the ceiling and turning over the recent events since public performances of my play *Ngaahika Ndeenda* had been banned, and that when I heard the knocking at the door and put on my shoes and went to the window and saw uniformed police officers, I felt as if I had been expecting the scene all along.

This I could not tell him, even if I had had the necessary energy or desire, because a few seconds after his query, some other police came for me, put me in another car, and drove me away. These were not among the ones who arrested me, and they didn't utter a word to me or to each other. It was only after what seemed an eternity that we reached another police station. Kīambu!

The same ritual. Into an empty room, in silence. They leave and I hear them lock the door from the outside. I was not alone for very long. A tall slim man came in and, still standing, staring straight ahead, almost past me, made the formal announcement:

"I am Superintendent Mbūrū attached to Kīambu Police Station, and I am under instructions to arrest and place you in detention. Have you anything to say?"

The whole exercise, executed in an emotionless tone, had a slightly comic side: So between Limuru and Kīambu I was not under police arrest?

"Do your duty!" was all I said.

He didn't handcuff me. As he walked me toward a yellow Volvo not marked with police colors, an onlooker would have thought that he and I were old friends. Mbūrū drove; I sat in the passenger seat next to him. I almost relaxed at the respite from the show of armed terror! Mbūrū even started a conversation:

"Did your family originally come from the Rift Valley?" he asked.

"No!" I said.

"I have had that impression from reading your books."

"I only write about it," I said.

It was so casual, so ordinary, that it felt as though Mbūrū was only giving me a lift to Nairobi instead of taking me to an unknown destination.

Then the ordinariness of the situation began to disturb me.

He and I were alone in the car. Though in civilian clothes, he was still a police officer, an agent of the state. He was armed, it was night, and there were no other vehicles on the road. Suddenly, what had once happened to Josiah Mwangi Kariũki crossed my mind. On March 2, 1975, JM, a prominent populist nationalist, was taken by police from a Nairobi Hotel in the daytime, and his body was later found mutilated in Ngong Forest. Could Mbũrũ be on a similar mission?

My wife knew only that I had been taken by Tigoni police. The Tigoni police knew only that they had handed me to Kĩambu police. And the police who brought me to Kĩambu hadn't even seen Mbũrũ walk me to the car. The breaks in the chain of custody began to seem eerily sinister. None of those in that chain could ever tell more than they knew. And now there was no eyewitness to anything that might happen to me. The torturous thoughts ended only when I saw him stop at Kilimani Police Station, in Nairobi, the capital city.

The following morning—it was now Saturday, the last day of 1977—a Mr. Munene Mũhĩndĩ, who I later came to learn was an assistant commissioner of police in charge of the Nairobi area and also the political prisoners' security officer, served me with detention orders. No sooner did he leave than some police came in and suddenly grabbed me and roughly put me in chains. I was then shoved from behind into the backseat of a blue car between two hefty police officers armed with a machine gun and a rifle, while a third one, equally well equipped, sat in the front seat beside the driver. Blinds were drawn on all sides except the back, but anybody looking would have seen only the police officers, not the prisoner sandwiched between them. They drive through the heavy traffic in Nairobi to the gates of the infamous Kamĩtĩ Maximum Security Prison.

The driver almost smashed his way through the heavy closed outer doors of the giant prison. Realizing his mistake, he quickly backed into a small bush, under a tree, car blinds still drawn, so that none of the people walking about could see who or what was inside the Black Maria.

The whole area around Kamĩtĩ was put under curfew—suddenly at noon! I saw innocent men, women, and children dive for cover pursued by baton-waving prison guards, and within seconds, there was not a single civilian standing or walking in the vicinity. The poor folk had unknowingly made the mistake of peacefully going about their daily chores during the ceremony of detention and imprisonment and no doubt paid for the pleasure with a few bruises here and there. I had last seen such a scene in colonial Kenya during the barbaric State of Emergency when similar terror tactics were a daily occurrence.

Even the huge prison gates, which, like the jaws of a ravenous monster, now slowly swung open to swallow me, reminded me of the colonial past. Those walls still dripped with the blood of the many Kenyan nationalists, fighters, and supporters of the Kenya Land and Freedom Army, derisively labeled Mau Mau by the colonial settler state. They had died as mere numbers on prison files. Even now, still belonging to nameless numbers, their bones, including Dedan Kĩmathi's,[13] lie in that foul place, unwept and unremembered by ungrateful inheritors of the power they paid for with their lives. They had lost their names, forever.

Ironies of history: it was now my turn. From Saturday

December 31, 1977, I had died to my name of Ngũgĩ wa
Thiong'o. Henceforth I would only answer to a lifeless number on a file among many files. K6,77 was my new identity.

6

Later I would learn that for two weeks after my abduction,
my family and the nation were kept in ignorance of my fate.
Every police and government official pleaded ignorance until
my detention was announced in the *Kenya Gazette* of January 6, 1978 (though this issue was held and not released until
January 14).

Even then my whereabouts remained a secret known only
to an initiated few. The government went to ridiculous lengths
to hide all our whereabouts, like convening the Detainees
Review Tribunal in Mombasa and flying the political prisoners there. Yet virtually all the members of the tribunal
were transported from Nairobi, only ten minutes' drive from
Kamĩtĩ. Or like the mystery surrounding a political prisoner's
meeting with family at Embakasi Airport, Nairobi, giving the
family the impression that their prisoner son had been flown
there from afar. For the duration of the visit, a police officer
was present. And whenever a political prisoner went out and
came in, curfew was clamped on the entire prison.

Why all the mystery, the suspense, the secrecy? Did they
really fear that people would storm Kamĩtĩ Prison to free
political prisoners by force?

The ruling clique knows it has a monopoly of all the instruments of coercive violence, but it also knows that no force on

earth can finally put down the organized power of an awakened people—hence the imperative to raise people in a culture of fear and silence,[14] to make them feel weak and helpless before the might of the state. The state assumes the malevolent character of a terrifying supernatural force that can be placated only by the supplications of a people on their knees, appeased only by the sacrifice of human flesh by assassinations, as in the cases of Pio Gama Pinto[15] and J. M. Kariũki,[16] both progressive nationalists.

The rituals of mystery and secrecy are calculated exercises in psychological terror aimed both at the whole people—part of the culture of fear—and at individual political prisoners—part of the strategy to break them. The first is harder to see, for it can only be understood by delving into history, our history, to trace the roots of the current ruling-class culture. That will come later. It is to understand it that I am writing this account. The latter is easier to see, however, for it is part of the daily trials of a political prisoner.

The rituals, seemingly petty and childish but rigorously followed to the letter by decorated guards and bemedaled officers, serve to make political prisoners feel that they have been completely cut off from the people and hence from group solidarity—the sense of being one with the people—which alone keeps men and women going, even when menaced by truncheons, nailed boots, tear gas, and death whistling bullets. They must be made, not just to know, but to actually feel that, with the links cut, they are now adrift in an ocean of endless fear and humiliation. They are not introduced into the ocean gradually. They are thrown into it to swim and stay afloat any way they know—or plunge into the depths and drown.

In the first month, I was locked up in cell 16 for twenty-two hours every day. The remaining two hours were distributed to cover the daily chores of emptying the chamber pot full to the top with shit and urine; gulping down the breakfast, lunch, and supper of porridge, *ugali* corn meal and beans; and getting sunshine and exercise. How had the other political prisoners coped with these conditions? I would ask myself. How had they managed to stay afloat?

For the first three weeks of that month, I was also under internal segregation. This simply meant that no other political prisoner was allowed near me. During meals, I was made to sit apart from the others, often with a guard between us. During my ration of sunshine, I had to sit in my corner, often with a watchful guard to ensure that there was no talking or other contact between me and any of the others.

Because we were all in the same block, it wasn't easy for the warders to enforce total segregation. The other political prisoners would break through the cordon by shouting across to me or by finding any and every excuse for going past where I was sitting and hurriedly throwing in one or two words of solidarity. Or they might assure me of their solidarity as they walked past my cell—the other political prisoners were let out for sunshine in groups of twos or threes for short periods, and a few for much longer periods, though no more than three of them were allowed into the yard at once, on doctor's orders. This was always very touching coming from people who were in no better conditions.

Sometimes two political prisoners would stand just far enough away not to be accused of being with me but near enough for me to hear everything. They would talk to each other about various aspects of prison life, sometimes offering advice or hints on how to cope, but I knew that this was meant for me. And at night, or when inside our cells in the day, there was no way of preventing the others from shouting messages and anecdotes through the walls or keep me from shouting back news of what had been happening in the world up to the time of my arrest.

Despite the best efforts of my fellow political prisoners to break the walls of segregation, however, the feeling of being alone would often steal into me, and I would be seized with the momentary panic of a man drowning in a sea of frothy terror. I often felt like lepers in medieval Europe, who had to carry small bells around their necks to announce their leprous presence to the healthy, or the Osu, the Untouchables, well portrayed in Chinua Achebe's novels, who had to jump into the bush to let a freeborn pass. In my case, I was being denied the social fellowship of even the other political untouchables.

Months later, when I told the other political prisoners about my feelings during those weeks of January, they laughed and told me how lucky I was to have had them around me, that the sense of isolation is a thousand times more intense for those in solitary confinement.

Mūhoro wa Mūthoga, popularly known as Fujika, told me that his own initiation into prison life at Kamĩtĩ was through a six-month solitary confinement in a ghostly cell in what was known as the isolation block. Every effort was exerted to make him live and feel the reality behind that phrase. His only contacts were the guards who brought him food, let him out for an hour of sunshine and exercise, and guarded the empty silent corridors. One guard always walked on tiptoe. Another would open the cell door, push food inside, and then jump back quickly, shutting the door as if the inmate were a dangerous animal in a cage. Yet another guard, the most liberal, would speak to him words through clenched teeth as if the words were being painfully pulled out of his tongue at some cost, and even then the words would come out as whispers. Otherwise the others communicated with him only in gestures.

He started doubting himself: Could he possibly and unknowingly have done something more terrible than just asking for application forms from the attorney general to legally register a new democratic political party? Could he have misread the Kenyan constitution, which, on paper at least, allowed more than one political party? The application forms had been sent to him, all right. He had sent the forms back with the constitution of the intended party. In answer, he was arrested and sent to Kamĩtĩ Maximum Security Prison. Maybe *intentions* to form new political parties to represent classes other than the comprador[17] bourgeoisie had been banned, and he had failed to read the relevant gazette! He told me that he always felt as if he was under a death sentence, awaiting execution.

Gradually he grew into the habit of also speaking in whispers or gesturing whenever he wanted to ask for something. On a few occasions, he caught himself walking on tiptoe, even when alone. When he was finally let out of the six-month ordeal and met the others in the main detention block, he was really scared of them, as if they were beings from another world. He started speaking to them in whispers!

I was never subjected to this form of torture. My own initiation into prison life took the psychological form of internal segregation. Nevertheless, the constant reminder of my social apartness, this cruel human isolation in the midst of fellow humans, a case really of water everywhere and not a drop to drink, began to tell on me. I became edgy. Voices of guards, even when seemingly friendly, would grate on my nerves unpleasantly; murderous thoughts would suddenly seize me. Fortunately for me (and others), these thoughts found no physical expression. But soon they found an outlet in words!

7

The first verbal "victim" was the prison chaplain, who one morning came into my cell staggering under the weight of two huge Bibles—*The Living Bible* in English and *Ibuku Rĩa Ngai* (*The Holy Bible*) in Gĩkũyũ—plus a bundle of revivalist tracts from the American-millionaire-rich evangelical missions. He was in a prison officer's uniform of khaki trousers and jumper coat with aluminum buttons and a decoration of two or three stones on the shoulder flaps. He also carried the hallmark of all prison officers and warders—a cord over the left shoulder carrying a whistle hidden in the breast pocket. Underneath these symbols of oppression, he wore the holy uniform of a reverend: a black cloak with a white collar around the neck. I held my tongue and let him talk.

"Sometimes," he said, after sitting on the edge of the desk seat with me on the bed, "God chastises us for our own good. . . . Take Mau Mau, for instance. . . . Mau Mau was God's scourge with which he lashed Kenyans to teach them a good lesson. . . . The fruit of this lesson, well learnt, is the stability we now enjoy and which is the envy of our neighbors."

I could hardly believe my ears: KLFA, the Kenya Land and Freedom Army, or Mau Mau, as the British called the soldiers of liberation, who, with their sacrifice and courage, wrote the most glorious chapter in our nation's long history of struggle, was to this man with the cloak of a priest beneath a prison officer's uniform, a huge *sjambok* (whip) with which God flagellated Kenyans into humble submission to his eternal will.

"We have all sinned and come short of the glory of God," he said. "Who knows, maybe this is a unique God-created chance for you to meet with Christ." He went on: "God works in mysterious ways, his wonder to perform,"

He didn't see the anger seething inside me. In my silence, he could see only a being about to be smitten to the ground by the thunderbolt of the Lord, like Saul in the New Testament. But to me, his attempts at verbal comfort sounded like prayers of thanksgiving for being chosen to be the earthly instrument of God's mysterious ways of performing his wonders, and his attempts at converting me were trumpets of victory over a fallen foe of imperialist Christendom.

My silence lured him on. He now presented me with the two Bibles.

"The Bible is the only book in the world containing within its hard covers a complete library," he said, fingering each Bible lovingly as he placed it on the desk. "Sixty-six books in one . . . how many people can boast of a home library that big?"

He then handed me two religious tracts—one of which was *God's City in Heaven* or some such title—with obvious awe at the American-manufactured weightless leaves of holiness.

Despite my mounting anger, I beat a hasty retreat from his verbal onslaught and actually took the leaves. I really felt weak before the moral certainty of a man who had walked the same path over and over again and hence knows every sharp corner and dangerous bend, every nook and brook on the way, a man who knows clearly, from years of experience, where this path leads to: a prisoner's acceptance to carry the cross forever without a murmur of discontent, because he now has the spiritual satisfaction of having Christ for a personal savior.

The visit had been beautifully timed. For over two weeks now, I had not engaged in any debate; indeed, I had hardly talked to anyone at any length since the night I was abducted from home. I had been denied human company. At the time of his visit, all the older political prisoners except Martin Shikuku, had gone to Shimo La Tewa Prison in Mombasa to meet the review tribunal. I was totally alone. I felt as if I were on the run, relentlessly pursued by an invisible silent malignant force that, despite my every effort to outdistance it, had finally caught up with me and was now transforming me, a free agent able to make decisions, into a passive creature panting and cringing for mercy at the feet of the twin warders of body and soul. My hard anger had now melted into a kind of spiritual lethargy and intellectual torpidity. What's the point of talking back? Isn't it easier, for me, for everybody, but mostly for me, to buy peace with silence?

The priest sensed the uncertainty in his quarry. He now took out his spiritual dagger and went for the kill.

"Let us kneel down and ask God for forgiveness for all our sins," he commanded—but in a voice tear-bathed in infinite pity and compassion.

Then suddenly, from somewhere in the depths of my being, rose a strong rebellious voice. It said, "Wake up from your spiritual lethargy and intellectual torpor. Don't let them drug you with this stuff; don't let them poison your system with it. It was to make you acutely hunger and thirst for a compassionate human voice that they have kept you near and yet far from human company. If you let him get away with this, you are going to be his prisoner for the rest of your stay here and possibly forever."

I felt life stir.

"Hold it!" I cried out. "Who needs your prayers, your Bibles, your leaves of holiness—all manufactured and packaged in America? Why do you always preach humility and acceptance of sins to the victims of oppression? Why is it that you never preach to the oppressor? Go. Take your Bibles, your prayers, your leaves of holiness to them who have chained us in this dungeon. Have you read *Ngaahika Ndeenda*? Did you ever go to see the play? What was wrong with it? Tell me! What was wrong with Kamĩrĩthũ peasants and workers wanting to change their lives through their own collective efforts instead of always being made passive recipients of *harambee,* the-all-pull-together-slogan of charity meant to buy peace and sleep for uneasy heads? Tell me truthfully: what drove you people to suppress the collective effort of a whole village? What has your Christianity to say to oppression and exploitation of ordinary people?"

I was getting worked up. A few guards crowded the door, but I didn't care. I flayed, right to its rotten roots, his spiritual dependence on imperial foreigners. What had made him bring me tracts written by Billy Graham? Didn't he know that this was the same man who used to bless American soldiers on their missions to napalm, bomb, murder, and massacre Vietnamese men, women, and children in the name of an anti-communist holy crusade? Were there no Kenyans who could write sermons? Why hadn't he at least paid homage to Kenya's spiritual independence by bringing into prison sermons by the likes of Reverend John Gatū[18] and Bishop Henry Okullu, men whose liberal sincerity and concern had led them to a measure of patriotism?

My denunciatory vehemence shook him. He became defensive. The moral certainty had gone. Avoiding the earthly issues of oppression, exploitation, and foreign control, he said that as a man of God he never indulged in politics. To justify that stand, he quoted the Biblical exhortation to believers to "render unto Caesar things that are Caesar's and unto God the things that are God's." I quickly quoted back to him the Biblical scene in which Jesus whipped out of God's earthly temple the Pharisee and Sadducee collaborators with Caesar's oppressive rule.

A little game started. He would refer me to Biblical passages that talked of faith, sin, salvation, grace, and life after death; I would in turn refer him to alternative passages in which God is cited as having sent his prophets to denounce earthly misrule and oppression of innocents.

He abruptly cut short the heated exchange. "Anyway, we could go on arguing forever, but I have others to see. You educated people like arguments too much. But remember that you cannot argue your way to Heaven."

He stood up, took back the two huge Bibles and the bundle of Billy Graham, and staggered toward cell 11, where Martin Shikuku was on a hunger strike.

The second verbal "victim" was a guard. He was on leave

when I was brought to Kamĩtĩ. This was his first shift since resuming work. Suddenly, out of the blue, he shouted at me and accused me of dragging my feet in returning to my cell. "We know what you're trying to do, but don't be too clever. This is not the university," he added, wagging a warning finger at me. This was soon after our supper, usually eaten at 3:00 p.m.

The political prisoners and even the other guards turned their heads toward us.

They knew that he had deliberately picked on me as an object on which to display his talents in bullying. Total silence in Kamĩtĩ. Everybody froze into his position to better absorb the drama as it unfolded.

The kind of lethargy I had earlier felt before the spiritual warder again crept in, to still my trembling anger: "I am new in this place. . . . Shouldn't I buy peace by simply swallowing my anger and pride and slink into my cell? I am down. I must avoid confrontation."

But another voice, the other voice, quickly intervened: "You may be down now, but you must always struggle to rise. Struggle for your rights. If you don't pick up the glove, if you don't stand to your full height now and stare injustice in the face, you'll never be able to raise your head in this place. It's now or never!"

I stood up. But instead of going back to the cell, I walked toward the new guard in slow, measured steps. I tried to speak in a controlled voice but loud enough for everybody to hear. I wanted to be firm without shouting.

"You know very well that you did not tell me to go back to my cell. You also know that it is not yet time to go in. To me, even a second of my ration of sunshine is precious and it is my right. I am not begging for more than my due, and I have no intention of doing so in future. But whatever the case, never, never shout at me or abuse me. If I have broken any regulation, do your duty and tell me so politely. I will hear. If I refuse to obey, you should report me to your superiors: the corporal, the sergeant, the chief, officer one, the superintendent, or the senior superintendent. But don't add tyranny to the insult and injury of lies and falsehoods."

He looked about him for support from the other guards. No voice or gesture came to his rescue. Suddenly noise and movement returned to the compound. We severally went back to our cells. It was an unwritten rule among political prisoners never to loudly comment on the results of a showdown between a political prisoner and a guard, especially when the political prisoner had won, for fear of uniting the guards into a common determination of vengeance. But I knew from the relaxed tone of their voices and the ease of their laughter that they were happy I had stood up to him.

"That warder is a well-known bully." In fact, Koigi wa Wamwere told me later, "If you hadn't answered back, he would have gone on to spit at you and shit on you. I would like you to watch how he treats political prisoner X, who, in order to avoid conflict, dances to their every whim and caprice."

Those two small incidents, and my own internal struggles to know how to react, brought home to me the real message behind what Wasonga Sijeyo had told me about my not letting them break me. They also showed me the tactical meaning behind all those mystificatory rituals.

It is this: prison and conditions in there, including the

constant reminder of one's isolation, are meant to make former patriots feel that they have been completely forgotten, that all their former words and actions linked to people's struggles were futile gestures and senseless acts of a meaningless individual martyrdom. Every aspect of prison is devised to reduce them to a condition in which they finally think, *The masses have betrayed me. Why should I sacrifice myself for them?*

For a detained patriot, breaking through the double walls of gray silence, attempting even a symbolic link with the outside world, is an act of resistance. And resistance—even at the level of merely asserting one's rights, of maintaining one's ideological beliefs in the face of a programmed onslaught—is in fact the only way political prisoners can maintain their sanity and humanity. Resistance is the only means of trying to prevent a breakdown. The difficulty lies in the fact that in this effort one must rely first and foremost on one's own resources (writing defiance on toilet paper for instance), and nobody can teach one how to do it.

All messages of solidarity, even through a silent photograph or an unwritten word in a letter, are important contributions to the struggle to stay afloat. To a person condemned to isolation, such messages from the outside sound like Joshua's trumpets, which brought down the legendary walls of Jericho.

True for me, too: Njoki, with a picture sent through the mail, and Warĩnga, with an image created on rationed toilet paper, have been more than a thousand trumpets silently breaking down the fortified walls of Kamĩtĩ Maximum Security Prison to assure me that I am not alone. Warĩnga, by constantly making me conscious of my connection with history, and Njoki, by constantly making me aware that I am now in prison because of Kamĩrĩthũ and its people, buoyed up my sagging spirits.

Warĩnga and Njoki also keep reminding me that my imprisonment without trial is not a personal affair. It's part of the wider history of attempts to bring up the Kenyan people in a reactionary culture of silence and fear, and of the Kenyan people's fierce struggle against them to create a people's revolutionary culture of outspoken courage and heroism. Despite independence, our status was still colonial. Well, a colonial affair.

2

Parasites in Paradise

1

The phrase *a colonial affair* carries hints of the Happy Valley period of the pioneering white settler between the 1920s and 1940s, which once provoked the sexually suggestive question, in Britain at least, "Are you married, or do you live in Kenya?"

The words keep intruding into the literary flow of my mind... a colonial affair in an independent Kenya.... It is as if the phrase has followed me inside Kamĩtĩ Prison to mock me.

In 1967, just before returning home from my three years at Leeds University, England, I signed a contract with William Heinemann to write a book on the social life of European settlers in Kenya. The literary agent who negotiated the contract—he was also the originator of the idea—put it this way: "Theirs is a world which has forever vanished, but for that very reason, many readers will find an account of it still interesting."

"A Colonial Affair" was the title under which I signed the contract. It was his, not mine, but it felt right.

I agreed to do the book because I strongly held that the

settlers were part of the history of the country: we could not ignore the seventy years of their destructive alien presence. I tried hard to come to terms with the task. I dug up old newspapers and settlers' memoirs to get an authentic feel of the times as the settlers lived it. The more I dug up the sordid details of their Happy Valley lifestyle, the more it disturbed me.

The Happy Valley was an actual area, Wanjohi Valley, around Naivasha, between Nairobi and Nakuru towns, but the name also described the lifestyle of a white landed idle class that killed boredom with hunting, alcohol, other drugs, temporary marriages, divorce, wife swapping, murders, and suicides. As a lifestyle, it encompassed the entire geographic area of initial white settlement, from Baron Delamere's Soysambu Ranch in Naivasha, thence forty miles to Nyeri, and another fifty or so to the Mūthaiga Country Club, the Norfolk Hotel, and the Karen District in Nairobi.

At the center of the Happy Valley crowd around Naivasha was one Josslyn Hay, twenty-second Earl of Erroll, whose company was sought by both men and women. All of the white women, particularly the married ones, wanted to bed him. In 1934, he joined the British Union of Fascists, which had been founded in 1932 by Sir Oswald Mosley, a friend and admirer of Benito Mussolini. In 1936, the BUF changed its name to the British Union of Fascists and National Socialists to more explicitly signal its alliance with Hitler, who was an honored guest at Mosley's wedding. Hay was BUF representative in Kenya, while simultaneously being the president of the settler policy body, the Convention of Associations. In his person and among the Happy Valley crowd, fascism and white settler supremacy became policy and way of life. As his family's peerage dated back to 1453, Hay truly brought "real royalty" to settler fascism in Kenya.

His affair with Lady Diana Delves Broughton ended with his murder in January 1941. Sir Jock Delves Broughton, Lady Diana's husband, was accused of murdering Hay. He was acquitted, however, only to commit suicide a year or so later. Lady Diana, who quickly divorced Broughton, ended up as Lady Diana Delamere, after she married Thomas Pitt Hamilton Cholmondeley, fourth Baron Delamere of Vale Royal. She outlived the members of the original set long enough to witness the transition of the country from white highlands to an independent black African country. In marrying Lord Delamere, inserting herself at the center of the royal family of white settlerdom, she ensured that the Happy Valley image[1] would outlive the colonial era into the postcolonial.[2]

In the end, despite the research, I was unable to write the book. I couldn't quite find the right tone. The difficulty lay in more than my uncertainty as to whether or not "their world" had really vanished. I couldn't just write about their debauchery and endless blood lust and leave it there. An account of their social life would have to include a section on culture, and I was by then convinced that a Draculan idle class could never produce a culture.

White settlers in Kenya were really parasites in paradise. The Right Honorable Hugh Cholmondeley, third Baron Delamere, Knight Commander of the Order of Saint Michael and Saint George—the father of "Tom" Delamere—best exemplifies this bloodsuckery. This lord transformed himself from a White Hunter of lions into a White Hunter of other people's lands. In 1903, he bagged a hundred thousand acres at Njoro, which he renamed Equator Ranch, and then fifty thousand more in and around Naivasha, which he renamed Soysambu. The words *lord*, *lion*, *land*, and *loot* begin with the same letter. Thus the knight commander of two saintly orders was the founding spirit of mass land robbery and of the not-too-saintly Happy Valley lifestyle. Maybe saints and sinners are two sides of the same coin. To him and those who followed him, Kenya was a huge winter home for English aristocracy, a place for big-game hunting and living it up on the backs of a million field and domestic slaves on lands stolen from them.[3]

"No one coming into a new country," Lord Cranworth wrote in his 1939 *Kenya Chronicles*, "could desire a more attractive welcome. . . . We were rowed ashore in a small boat and came to land on the shoulders of sturdy Swahili natives." Coming ashore into Kenya meant literally riding on the backs of black workers into a white tropical paradise, and this was true for the titled and the untitled alike.

By setting foot on Kenyan soil at Mombasa, every European, even those soldiers resettled on stolen lands after the First World War, was instantly transformed into a blue-blooded aristocrat. An attractive welcome: before him, stretching beyond the ken of his eyes, lay a vast valley garden of endless physical leisure and pleasure that he must have once read about in the *Arabian Nights* stories. The dream in fairy tales was now his in practice. No work, no winter, no physical or mental exertion. Here he would set up his own fiefdom.

Life in these fiefdoms is well captured in Gerald Henley's novels *Consul at Sunset* and *Drinkers of Darkness*. Whoring, hunting, drinking—why worry? Work on the land was done by gangs of African "boys." But these books are fiction, of course.

Documentary evidence comes from the records of a traveler. In her 1929–1930 diaries, later published together under the title *East African Journey*, Margery Perham described the same life in minute detail:

> We drove out past the last scattered houses of suburban Nairobi, houses very much like their opposite numbers in England. But here ordinary people can live in sunlight; get their golf and their tennis more easily and cheaply than at home; keep three or four black servants; revel in a social freedom that often turns, by all accounts, into licence, and have the intoxicating sense of belonging to a small ruling aristocracy.... Certainly, on the surface, life is very charming in Nairobi, and very sociable with unlimited entertaining; all the shooting, games and bridge anyone could want. And in many houses a table loaded with drinks, upon which you can begin at any hour from 10.00am onwards, and with real concentration from 6.00pm.

Beyond drinking whisky, drugging themselves into sexual fantasies, whoring each other's spouses, and gunning lions and natives for pleasure in this vast Happy Valley, the settlers produced little. No art, no literature, no culture, just the making of a little dominion marred only by niggers too many to exterminate, the way they did in America, New Zealand, and Australia, and threatened by upstart "African agitators."

The one who reached highest in creative literature was perhaps Elspeth Huxley, but she is better known as the literary apologist for white settlement with her voluminous historical polemic, *White Man's Country: Lord Delamere and the Making of Kenya*. The most creative things about her writing are her titles—*The Flame Trees of Thika* and *The Mottled Lizard*, for instance—because in them she allows herself to be inspired by native life and landscape. Beyond the title and the glossy covers, there is only defense of oppression, and defense of human oppression has never been a subject for great literature.

Their theater, professional and amateur, never went beyond crude imitation and desperate attempts to keep up with the West End and Broadway. The settlers never produced a single original script or actor or critic.

In science, they could of course display Louis Leakey, undoubtedly a great archaeologist. Leakey's specialty was in digging up, dating, and classifying old skulls. Like George Eliot's Casaubon, he was happier living with the dead. To the Leakeys, it often seemed that the archaeological ancestors of Africans were more lovable and noble than the current ones—an apparent case of regressive evolution. Colonel Leakey, and even Louis Leakey, readily proposed ways of killing off African nationalism, while praising skulls of dead Africans as precursors of humanity. L.S.B. Leakey is the author of two antiliberation polemics—*Mau Mau and the Kikuyu* and *Defeating Mau Mau* (i.e., the Kenya Land and Freedom Army.)

In art, the settler class's highest achievement was the murals on the walls of the Lord Delamere bar in the Norfolk Hotel, Nairobi.[4] The murals stand to this day, and they still attract hordes of tourists who come to enjoy racist aesthetics in art. Their artistic mediocrity only enhances their revealing historical realism.

On one wall are depicted scenes drawn from the English countryside: fourteen different postures for the proper deportment of an English gentleman; fox-hunting with gentlemen and ladies on horseback surrounded on all sides by well-fed hounds panting and wagging tails in anticipation of the kill to come; and of course the different pubs, from the White Hart to the Royal Oak, waiting to quench the thirst of the ladies and the gentlemen after their blood sports. Kenya is England away from England, with this difference: Kenya is an England of endless summer tempered by an eternal spring of sprouting green life.

On another wall are two murals depicting aspects of settler life in that Kenya. One shows the Norfolk—the House of Lords, as it was then known—in 1904. Here again are English ladies and gentlemen—some on horseback, others sitting or standing on the veranda, but all drinking hard liquor served them by an African waiter wearing the servant's uniform of white kanzu, red fez, and a red band over his shoulder and front. In the foreground is an ox wagon with two Africans: one, the driver, lashing at the dumb oxen, and the other, the pilot, pulling them along the right paths. The ribs of the "pushing boy" and the "pulling boy" are protruding, in contrast to the fully fleshed oxen and members of the House of Lords.

However, the most prominent feature in this mural is a "rickshaw boy" with grinning teeth, holding up this human-powered carriage for a finely dressed English lady to enter. Oxen-powered wagons for English survival goods;

African-powered carriages for the good English lords and ladies. Eleanor Cole, in her 1975 random recollections of pioneer settler life in Kenya, writes:

> Transport in Nairobi in those days was by rickshaw, one man in front between the shafts and one behind, either pushing or acting as a brake. People had their private rickshaws and put their rickshaw men in uniform. There were also public ones for hire.

The other mural depicts the same type of royal crowd at the Nairobi railway station. At the forefront is a well-fed dog wagging its tail before its lord and master. Amid the different groups chatting or walking stands a lone bull-necked, bull-faced settler in riding breeches with a hat covering bushy eyebrows and a gray moustache. He could have been a Colonel Grogan or a Lord Delamere or any other settler. The most representative feature about him is the *sjambok* he is firmly holding in his hands.

The rickshaw. The gun. The dog. The *sjambok*. The ubiquitous underfed, wide-eyed, uniformed native slaves, the grown men they called boys!

In March 1907, Colonel Ewart Grogan and four associates flogged three "rickshaw boys" outside a Nairobi courthouse. The "boys" were later taken to the hospital with lacerated backs and faces. Their crime? They had alarmed two white ladies by raising the rickshaw shafts an inch too high! The rhetoric of the magistrate, when Grogan, Russell Bowker, a Captain Gray, Sidney Fichat, and Ernest Low were summoned before him for being members of an unlawful assembly, left not the slightest doubt about the sadistic brutality of these sons of English nobility, graduates of Eton and Cambridge:

> From the first to the last it appears to me that out of all the people present assisting at the flogging of these men, there was no one of that number who ever took the trouble to satisfy himself as to whether these natives had ever done anything deserving of punishment at all. There was no trial of any sort nor any form or pretence of trial. These boys were neither asked whether they had any defence or explanation to give, nor does it appear that they ever had any opportunity of making one. Grogan, who ordered the flogging, has himself stated that no plea or defence which they might have made would have diverted him from his purpose. This is a very unpleasant feature in the case and I consider it about as bad as it can be. Yet, in my opinion, it is further aggravated by the fact that the place selected for this unlawful act was directly in front of a court-house.

Correct legal rhetoric versus mockery of justice: the culprits, all found guilty, were given prison terms ranging from seven to thirty days. Prison? Their own houses, where they were free to receive and entertain guests! Elsewhere, in the plantations and estates, the bwana (boss) would simply have shot and buried them—or fed them to his dogs.

In 1960, Peter Harold Poole shot and killed Kamawe Musunge for throwing stones at Poole's dogs in self-defense.

To the settlers, dogs ranked infinitely higher than Kenyans; Kenyans were either children, to be paternalistically loved, like dogs, but not appreciated, or mindless scoundrels, to be flogged or killed. In his autobiography, *Words*, Sartre has made the apt comment that "when you love children and dogs too much, you love them instead of adults." The settlers' real love was for dogs and puppies. A Kenyan defending against an attacking dog was a crime worse than a Brit murdering a Kenyan. When Poole was sentenced to death, the whole colonial Herrenvolk cried in unison against this "miscarriage of justice." Peter Harold Poole had done what had been the daily norm since 1895.

In 1918, for instance, two British peers flogged a Kenyan to death and later burned his body. His crime? He was suspected of having an intention to steal property. The two murderers were found guilty of a "simple hurt" and were fined £100 each. The governor later appointed one of them a member of a district committee to dispense justice among the natives. The gory details are there in W. McGregor Ross's book *Kenya from Within*. What he describes is the justice of the *sjambok*!

I thought about this in my cell at Kamĩtĩ Prison and suddenly realized that I had been wrong about the British settlers. The colonial system *did* produce a culture.

But it was the culture of hedonism without morality, a culture of legalized brutality, a racist ruling-class culture of fear, the culture of an oppressing minority desperately trying to impose total silence on a restive oppressed majority. This culture was sanctified by the very structure and practice of the colonial administration of governors, provincial and district commissioners, and officers right down to the askari (native police and soldiers). Prisons and police stations were the central support pillars of the lifestyle of parasites in paradise. I should have written that book: *Fear and Silence: A Colonial Affair.*

2

The culture of fear and silence: the diaries and memoirs of the leading intellectual lights of the old colonial system contain full literary celebration of this settler culture. We need go no further than Colonel Meinertzhagen's *Kenya Diaries* and Baroness Blixen's *Out of Africa.*

Richard Meinertzhagen was a commanding officer of the British forces of occupation, but he is far better known in history as the assassin of Koitalel Arap Samoei, the otherwise unconquerable military and political leader of the Nandi people. Under Koitalel's inspiring leadership, the Nandi people waged a ten-year armed struggle against the foreign army of occupation, humiliating British officers, one after the other. Enter Meinertzhagen, a gentleman. Unable to defeat the Nandi guerrilla army, the colonel invited Koitalel to a peace parley on some "neutral" ground. But only on one condition. Both men would come unarmed. Having been led to believe that the British wanted to discuss surrender terms and guarantees of safe retreat from Nandi country, Koitalel accepted. Pit innocence against brutality, and innocence will lose. Koitalel stretched an empty hand in greeting. Meinertzhagen stretched out a hidden gun and shot Koitalel in cold blood. The incident is recorded in *Kenya Diaries* as an act of British heroism!

Other such deeds of British colonial heroism are recorded in the same diaries.

The scene now shifts to Gĩkũyũ country, where once again people fought with tremendous courage against the better-armed foreign invaders. So fierce was the struggle that in 1902 Meinertzhagen was forced to make the grudging but prophetic admission that, even if they triumphed over the people, this would be only a temporary victory: the British could never hold the country for more than fifty years. In one of several battles in Mũrang'a, a British officer was captured by the people's defense army in Mũrũka and was handed to the people for justice. The women drowned him in urine. Months later, Meinertzhagen's troops stealthily surrounded the Mũrũka ground on a market day, and he ordered a massacre of every soul—murder of unarmed men, women, and children.

"Every soul was either shot or bayonetted; we burned all huts and razed the banana plantations to the ground. Then I went home and wept for brother officer killed," Meinertzhagen wrote in his diary.

Baroness Karen Christenze Blixen-Finecke was the separated wife of the big game hunter–cum–settler Baron Bror Fredrik von Blixen-Finecke. From him she got no children but did get incurable syphilis. As if in compensation for unfulfilled desires and longings, the baroness turned Kenya into a vast erotic dreamland in which her several white lovers appeared as young gods and her Kenyan servants as usable curs. In her two books, *Shadows on the Grass* and *Out of Africa*, the animals are the dominant images in her portrayal of Africans. In the more famous book, *Out of Africa*, she celebrates a hideous colonial aesthetic in an account she titles "Kitosch's Story":

> Kitosch was a young Native in the service of a young white settler of Molo. One Wednesday in June, the settler lent his brown mare to a friend, to ride to the station on. He sent Kitosch there to bring back the mare, and told him not to ride her, but to lead her. But Kitosch jumped on to the mare, and rode her back, and on Saturday the settler, his master, was told of the offence by a man who had seen it. In punishment the settler, on Sunday afternoon, had Kitosch flogged, and afterwards tied up in his store, and here late on Sunday night Kitosch died.

The outcome of the trial in the High Court at Nakuru turned to rest solely on the intentions of the victim. It was decided by a hideous logic that Kitosch had actually wanted to die, and he was therefore responsible for his death. In the colonial European mind, it seemed that colonized natives had a fiendish desire for death that absolved white murderers:

> Kitosch had not much opportunity for expressing his intentions. He was locked up in the store, his message, therefore comes very simply, and in a single gesture. The night-watch states that he cried all night. But it was not so, for at one o'clock he talked with the Toto, who was in the store with him, because the flogging had made him deaf. But at one o'clock he asked the

Toto to loosen his feet, and explained that in any case
he could not run away. When the Toto had done as
he asked him, Kitosch said to him that he wanted to
die. . . . A little while after, he rocked himself from side
to side, cried: "I am dead"! and died.

Medical science was even dragooned to support the wish-
to-die theory. This was a psychological peculiarity of the African. He wants to die, and he dies. The settler was found guilty
of "grievous hurt." And for a "grievous hurt" to a Kenyan, the
foreign settler got two years in jail.

The fault is not Blixen's manner of telling the story—all
the details are there—but her total acceptance of the hideous
wish-to-die theory and her attempts to draw from it aesthetic
conclusions meant to have universal relevance and validity
about the nature of the African.

By this strong sense in him of what is right and deco-
rous, the figure of Kitosch, with his firm will to die,
although now removed from us by many years, stands
out with a beauty of its own. In it is embodied the fugi-
tiveness of wild things who are, in the hour of need,
conscious of a refuge somewhere in existence; who go
when they will; of whom we can never get hold.[5]

The African is an animal: the settler is exonerated. But I err
in saying the African was considered an animal. In reality they
loved the wild game more. Africans were worse than animals,
because they asserted their humanity in the very threats they
posed to settlerdom.

Galbraith Cole shot dead a Maasai national, again in cold blood. The subsequent trial was a prearranged farce, rehearsed to the letter and gesture by all three parties, prosecutor, judge, and murderer (all European, of course), in such a way that, in the records, the murdered Kenyan emerged guilty of armed provocation. But the settler was too arrogant to hide his murderous intentions behind a mask of lies. As later reported by Karen Blixen, this is how the farce reached a climax of absurdity:

> "It's not, you know, that we don't understand that you shot only to stop the thieves," the Judge said to Galbraith.
>
> "No," Galbraith said, "I shot to kill. I said that I would do so."
>
> "Think again, Mr. Cole", said the judge. "We are convinced that you only shot to stop them."
>
> "No, by God." Galbraith said, "I shot to kill."
>
> He was acquitted.

Meinertzhagen, the soldier–assassin–turned–writer, and Karen Blixen, the baroness of blighted bloom–turned–writer —theirs is a literary reflection of that colonial culture of silence and fear best articulated in a dispatch by an early governor, Sir Arthur Henry Hardinge, on 5 April 1897:

> Force and the prestige which rests on a belief in force, are the only way you can do anything with those people, but once beaten and disarmed they will serve you. Temporizing is no good. . . . These people must

learn submission by bullets—It's the only school; after that you may begin more modern and humane methods of education, and if you don't do it this year you will have to next, so why not get it over? . . . In Africa to have peace you must first teach obedience, and the only tutor who impresses the lesson properly is the sword.

Thus the above acts of brutality were not aberrations of wayward individuals but an integral part of colonial politics, philosophy, and culture. Violence to instill fear and impose silence was the very essence of colonial settler culture.

3

This culture reached its high noon between 1952 and 1962. These were the ten years when the sword and the bullet held unmitigated sway over every Kenyan. It was a period of mass trials, mass torture, and mass murder of Kenyans. So brutal were the workings of this culture that some democratic-minded British were shocked into protest against its antihuman character.

Such was the case, for instance, of Eileen Fletcher, a Quaker social worker, who, after serving for a time as a rehabilitation officer in Kenya, resigned and flew back to England to declare in *The Tribune* magazine of May 25, 1956:

I have just come back from Kenya where I was sent by the British Government. I have seen Emergency

justice in operation. And now I can reveal the shock-
ing truth, that I have seen African children, in British
jails, sentenced to life imprisonment—for "consort-
ing with armed persons" and "unlawful possession of
ammunition." In a women's prison, less than a year
ago, I saw twenty-one young people—including 11 and
12 years olds—who were all condemned to this inhuman punishment, for supposed "Mau Mau offences."
All of them, believe it or not, had been convicted by
British magistrates.

Similarly, Barbara Castle, a Labour MP, had written in hor-
ror in *The Tribune* of September 30, 1955:

In the heart of the British Empire there is a police
state where the rule of law has broken down, where
the murder and torture of Africans by Europeans goes unpunished and where the authorities
pledged to enforce justice regularly connive at its
violation.

And in the *Sunday Pictorial* of March 31, 1957, after listing
nine Kenyans hanged in one night, she commented: "With
this bloody act, Kenya enters its fourth year of blood, repression, brutalities, mass imprisonment—of the lawless enforcement of unjust laws by agents of its government and of the
British Government."

Barbara Castle was, of course, wrong about what she termed
the breakdown of the rule of law. This *was* the rule of law, the

colonial rule of law, and it had been in operation, with differing degrees of intensity, since 1895.

Evidence comes from the horse's own mouth. On April 8, 1908, Secretary for Native Affairs Alfred Claud Hollis wrote a secret memorandum on the miserable conditions in the country's colonial labor camps:

> My first duty on my appointment as secretary for native affairs in June last was to inquire into the labour question. It had recently been reported to His Excellency that a number of Kikuyu had been found dead on the road leading from the railway fuel camps at Londiani to their country. I therefore proceeded to the spot and held an inquiry. A deplorable state of affairs was revealed. It transpired that as voluntary labour was usually not forthcoming, chiefs were called upon to provide labour, and natives were seized by their chief's orders and forced to go and work. The most unpopular kind of work was for Indian contractors on the railway. The men were sent to detested camps where they were badly fed and often beaten and maltreated. They frequently had no blankets given them though the cold at night time was intense, the miserable grass huts provided for their accommodation were neither watertight nor wind-proof, the work of felling trees and breaking stones was uncongenial, and no attempt was made to give them food they were accustomed to in their own homes. Their lives were consequently a misery and

their one idea seemed to be to run away and return to their own country. To prevent this, police guards were stationed at most of the contractor's camps. Many of the men however succeeded in escaping and hundreds must have died of starvation.

For some years a system of forced labor had been resorted to in various parts of the protectorate, and like most wrongful systems, it had gone from bad to worse. At first mild pressure only was used, then the goats were confiscated, and later on armed force had been employed.

It is indeed a tribute to the varied character of the human that even amid such carnage of body, mind, and truth, there are some courageous souls prepared to defy the conventionally accepted, speak truth to power, and risk arguing for our common humanity. In condemning racialized empires—or any empires—we must never forget those who stood up for a decent future for all even when it was unpopular or dangerous to do so.

Exactly thirty years before Barbara Castle, Marcus Garvey had to protest, in words similar to hers, against the 1922 British massacre of Kenyan workers when 150 women and men were mowed down outside the central police station for demanding the release of their jailed leader, Harry Thuku. Among the killers were members of the Happy Valley crowd shooting from the Delamere Terrace in the Norfolk Hotel. Marcus Garvey didn't see the massacre as a breakdown of law. He saw it as the logical working out of the laws of colonial conquest by the sword and the bullet. In a telegram to Lloyd George dated

March 20, 1922, which drew from a resolution passed in a mass meeting in Liberty Hall, Harlem, he prophesied a result that came to pass in 1952:

David Lloyd George British Premier Downing St London

Four-hundred million negroes through the Universal Negro Improvement Association hereby register their protest against the brutal manner in which your government has treated the natives of Kenya, East Africa. You have shot down a defenceless people in their own native land exercising their rights as men. Such a policy will aggravate the many historic injustices heaped upon a race that will one day be placed in a position to truly defend itself not with mere sticks, clubs and stones but with modern implements of science.

All these eruptions of brutality between the introduction of colonial culture in 1895 and its flowering in blood in the 1950s were not aberrations of an otherwise humane Christian culture. They were its very essence, its law, its logic—and the Kenyan settler, with his *sjambok*, his dog, his horse, his rickshaw, his sword, and his gun, was its true embodiment.

Barbara Castle and the antiwar activist Fenner Brockway were not the true representatives of the empire and the culture it was exporting and nurturing in the colonies. Its true representatives were Ewart Grogan, Baron Delamere, Richard Meinertzhagen, Francis Hall (a leader of military raids against the resisting Gĩkũyũ fighters), and the gun-toting Peter Poole. They alone understood and tenaciously clung to the primary goal of that culture—inducing submission by terror. They were impatient with the more deceitful methods of the missionaries and administrators, who were trying to educate Kenyans into submission. They differed in the method, not in the aims. No, at least these men were honest; in that fact lay their crude vigor and fascinating simplicity. They saw into the heart of their culture and understood and *embraced* its brutality, whereas others dressed the same predatory logic in biblical homilies, literary flourishes, and empty rhetoric about the rule of law.

Gabraith Cole, who shot the Maasai national, insisted he had shot to kill his victim, whereas the judge, the prosecutor, the defense counsel, and the jury were united in trying to find moral cover for themselves in declaring him innocent. In refusing to give them moral cover, Cole was more honest, for the hypocrites had to acquit him anyway. Of course, honesty doesn't absolve Cole of the crime; it just lets his actions and words open a window into the heartless heart of the entire colonial system.

Cole and his lot knew that the law was *their* law, not anybody else's, written to protect *their* interests by suppressing those of Kenyans, and they said it openly.

Long before Meinertzhagen came onto the scene with a sugar-coated bullet, a British military commander named Jackson tried and failed to subdue Koitalel's Nandi army. Jackson became almost insane and equated political defiance and military resistance with savagery. In a dispatch of

May 4, 1897, he tried to cover his military humiliation with words, which nevertheless reveal the "aesthetic" goals of that culture—submission, acceptance, and silence.

> I have carefully investigated, as far as possible, the reasons for their restlessness and it appears the great cause of the trouble is the hostile attitude assumed by the Chief Lybon, or medicine-man against the government. This man, who has apparently enormous influence over the various surrounding tribes, has declared (war) against the government, and is now busying himself in exhorting the tribes to expel the British. From reliable native information, I find he is endeavouring to bring about a movement against the administration, and numerous pieces of information clearly indicate that combined hostile action against us will undoubtedly begin on the cessation of the present rainy season. The Lybon has lately taken to sending insolent and defiant messages to the Fort, and the fact that no action has hitherto been taken against him has a very bad effect in the eyes of the natives, who say we are afraid of him. I have used every effort to conciliate the tribes and have exercised the greatest forbearance in dealing with them, and at their own request have even gone so far as to make blood brotherhood with many of them; but the ignorance of the people is so extreme that *it is impossible to convey to such savages that the occupation of their country is not harmful to them.* [italics mine]

Really, Mr. Jackson! Would you have said with similar equanimity that the occupation of Britain by Hitler's Germany would not have been harmful to Britons? In the same way, Hitler was surprised at the savage ignorance of other Europeans to whom it was impossible to convey that the occupation of their countries by blue-eyed blond vampires was not harmful to them.

4

The oppressed were to obey the oppressor. There was to be peace and harmony between the exploited and the exploiter. Slaves were to love the master and pray that God grant the master a long reign over them. These were the ultimate goals of colonial culture imposed by nailed boots, truncheons, and bayonets and carefully nurtured by the carrot of a personal heaven for a select few. The end was to teach Kenyans the beauty of submission and blind obedience to authority, reflected in the refrain of the Christian hymn "Trust and Obey":

> Trust and obey,
> For there's no other way
> To be happy in Jesus
> But to trust and obey!

Revelry in their own slavery: it was an ethic meant to make Kenyans readily accept, in the words of Jackson, that the occupation of their country by foreigners was not harmful to them.

Even in the 1950s, the colonial authorities were still busy

trying to educate Kenyans into accepting Jackson's ethic. In his book *Mau Mau Detainee*, J.M. Kariũki has described the kind of education they were being given in concentration camps:

> Attend education classes in their compound. These consisted mainly of the history of Kenya, with especial emphasis on the terrible state of tribal conflict before the arrival of the white man, followed by the story of the arrival of the white man and how he has saved us from barbarism, and finally an explanation of the great benefits he has brought to our country, especially in recent years.

Great benefits indeed! Kenyans received the sword and the bullet, got blood, repression, brutality, and starvation, watched the country's wealth carted off to keep Britain Great, and in return were expected to rejoice or cower in fear and silence.

3

Colonial Lazarus Rises from the Dead

1

Detention without trial had always been central to the colonial culture of fear. As early as 1897, barely two years after the East Africa Protectorate (Kenya) was established, the commissioner, Sir Arthur Hardinge—the philosopher of control by sword and the bullet—armed himself with powers of preventive detention and restriction of movement of any Kenyan disaffected with the government, or one about to commit an offense against the state, or any conducting themselves in a manner deemed by the colonial regime to be dangerous to peace and good order. There was no appeal against the governor's exercise of those powers. Thus was laid the legal groundwork for the fascist tradition of crimes of thought and intention.[1]

But even before colonial fascism was given its legal cover and formulation, it was already in operation, and it had claimed the freedom and lives of many Kenyan leaders. Waiyaki wa Hinga, the leading figure in the resistance against the British invasion and occupation of southern Gĩkũyũland—Kabete, as the Kĩambu District was then known—was among the earliest victims of preventive detention.

Waiyaki was one of several chiefs who were emerging toward feudal lordship status in Gĩkũyũland in the nineteenth century. But Waiyaki also loved his country. Combining political shrewdness and military brilliance, he and his army for many years thwarted British attempts to penetrate and occupy Dagoretti, Gĩthĩga, and Gĩthũngũri, eventually overrunning fortifications at Kĩawariũa. The British were forced to evacuate but managed a safe retreat with the guidance of the treacherous Kĩnyanjui wa Gathirimũ, later rewarded for this betrayal of his people by being made "their" paramount chief. The British forces came back in larger numbers and built Fort Smith, a bigger and stronger garrison, at Kanyarĩrĩ near the present Kikuyu station. Immediately Waiyaki's army besieged Fort Smith. W.P. Purkiss, the commanding officer, now resorted to that ol' British colonial treachery, which proved fatal to many a Kenyan nationalist whenever they assumed the colonials were dealing with honorable men. He invited Waiyaki to peace talks and had him arrested inside Fort Smith on August 14, 1892. Though now alone and surrounded by bayonets and Maxim guns, Waiyaki resisted and even bloodied one of his captors.

They could have killed him there and then, but he was more valuable to them as a hostage. The British plan worked. Waiyaki's army lifted the siege of Fort Smith.

Without scruples, the British decided to keep him a political hostage: on August 17, they sent him to detention in a prison on the coast. This too worked. Waiyaki's army held back, fearing that any action would bring injury to their beloved leader.

Then the British saw his value as a permanent hostage. Thinking that no native from the interior would ever know the truth, they shot Waiyaki and buried him, still breathing, still alive, at Kibwezi. It was sadistic sport, but his killers didn't know that some *hingas*[2] had followed the convoy and were sending back intelligence reports.

Waiyaki's arrest and murder rekindled the fire of militant nationalism and resistance. His army regrouped and laid another siege of Fort Smith. A visitor to the fort, Sir Gerald Portal, later wrote:

> At Kikuyu the European in charge dare not venture from the stockade without an armed escort of at least 30 to 50 men with rifles. He is practically a prisoner with all his people; and maintains the company's influence and prestige by sending almost daily looting and raiding parties to burn the surrounding villages and to seize the crops and cattle for the use of the company's caravans and troops.

Pillage, plunder, and murder. That was the colonial way. But that's another bunch of atrocities. Here we are looking at the early political prisoners and the traditions and forces they embodied in their actions and lives. Waiyaki, one of the first political prisoners in Kenya, was also among the first to die in detention. To the very end, he remained splendidly proud and defiant. Clearly he had rejected an enslaved consciousness!

Ngunju wa Gakere was another. He was the leading force in the struggle against the British occupation of Nyeri. He fought brilliant battles against the invaders, compelling

Meinertzhagen to admit in his diary that "I never expected the Wakikuyu to fight like this." On December 6, 1902, during a fierce battle to capture Nyeri Fort and dislodge the enemy forces, father (Gakere) and son (Ngunju) were captured. Ngunju wa Gakere was deported to Kismayu from 1902 to 1905. Then he was transferred to Mbiri, in Mũrang'a, where he died, in 1907. Like Waiyaki and Koitalel before him, he rejected an enslaved consciousness and remained proud and defiant to the end, thus joining the long line of resistance heroes leading to Kĩmathi in the 1950s.

Kenyan women played their part, too, and the most remarkable of them all was Me Katilili, the leader of the Giriama people's resistance to the British occupation. She was already advanced in years when she organized Giriama youth into a fighting force that took the British military machine three years to subdue. Old as she was, she saw very clearly the political character of the armed struggle. After talking to them about the theft of their land and labor and other evils of foreign occupation, she emphasized that the only solution was a united people's armed struggle against the foreign enemy.

She set up her own government and installed Wanji wa Mandoro as its head. She administered oaths of loyalty and unity among the Giriama people and then between them and the other related nationalities to forge oneness behind her administration. In the anti-imperialist oathing ceremonies, the youth swore loyalty to her government. They pledged to never again pay taxes to the colonial regime or accept the call of forced labor and swore to remain steadfast and unwavering in their aim to drive out the British enemy from coastal Kenya.

Inspired by her vision and courage, the Giriama fought so bravely that the British, refusing to see the political basis of this unity and courage, could only describe this remarkable feat in supernatural terms. Me Katilili had to be a witch who cast a spell over her primitive followers. Otherwise, how could Kenyans find the nerve to reject foreign rule, domination, and oppression? This would seem to have been the outlook of the assistant district commissioner, Arthur M. Champion, who on November 23, 1913, wrote thus to his superiors:

> The witch Me Kitilili and the witch-doctor Wanji wa Mandoro about the end of June, 1913, did stir up sedition amongst the natives of Gallana and Marafa in the district of Malindi and with this object held a large gathering of men determined to make a common cause with disaffected natives of Biria to meat a spell or "Kiroho" for the purpose of defeating a successful government administration. . . . When arrested, Wanji wa Mandoro asserted that he had been appointed chief elder of the Gallana to take precedence over all government appointed headmen. He further asserted that . . . he had held his own council of elders who came from all parts of Gallana to discuss matters and try cases, and that they took fees. . . . I would therefore recommend that both the woman Me Kitilili and Mandoro be deported from the district and be detained as political prisoners at His Majesty's pleasure.

The two were detained in November 1913 and deported to Gusiiland, hundreds of miles from the coast, where they faced death by starvation and cold.

C.E. Spenser, the colonial district commissioner of what was then South Kavirondo, was sufficiently moved by their miserable prison conditions to appeal to the provincial commissioners of Kisumu and Mombasa to ease the torture:

> These prisoners are old and unable to maintain themselves. I would suggest that they be allowed 10 cents a day each to provide themselves with food. . . . I cannot very well return the blankets they are wearing to Mombasa prison until they have been provided with others as I conceive that to leave them without covering in an altitude of 5,500 above sea-level, after a lifetime at the coast, would be equivalent to passing a death sentence on them.

Now comes an even more remarkable feat by this woman. On January 14, 1914, Me Katilili and her fellow political prisoner escaped and, with help from friendly compatriots of the other Kenyan nationalities, walked all the way back to the coast to continue the resistance. Rewards were announced for any person or persons who would assist in the recapture of this brave Kenyan. She was eventually caught on August 7, 1914, and imprisoned again. Me Katilili rejected the colonial culture of fear and the enslaved consciousness it sought to instill in Kenyans. She remained proud, defiant, and unrepentant to the very end.

The detention saga of Arap Manyei, the son of the legendary Koitalel, extends from 1922 to 1962. Manyei had continued his father's tradition of uncompromising resistance to foreign domination and oppression. He worked tirelessly to forge political unity among the Nandi and the related Kalenjin peoples. He also sent out feelers for a possible alliance with Luo and Gusii nationalists. It is possible that he may have also tried a working alliance with Harry Thuku's East African Association. Right from the start, he saw the necessity for armed struggle and, toward that end, administered an oath binding the Nandi people with other nationalities to wage a new war to drive out the British from Kenya. He was, however, arrested at Kapsabet in 1922 and was locked up in a prison in Meru for ten years.

He was unrepentant. In the 1950s, he established contact with the Kenya Land and Freedom Army. He started oathing and training parallel Nandi guerrilla units. He was arrested and imprisoned on Mfangano Island in Lake Victoria from 1957 to 1962, just a year before independence. He too remained defiant to the end. Not for him the enslaved mentality of the colonial culture of fear.

Manyei's detention was an important link in a chain that stretches from those of the early militant leaders of the armed resistance at the turn of the century through those of the early nationalists in the 1920s and thence to the mass detention and imprisonment of Kenyans in general and especially alleged members of the Kenya Land and Freedom Army (Mau Mau) in the 1950s.

The legal link was the Emergency Powers Colonial Defence Order in Council of 1939, under which the colonial governor could imprison or deport and exclude anyone from Kenya without recourse to the legislature or the courts.

When Governor Evelyn Baring invoked this order on October 20, 1952, the colonial culture entered its high noon and flowered in blood. The regime embarked on a ten-year program of herding Kenyan peasants and workers into concentration camps, such as those in Mackinnon Road, Langata, Manyani, Mageta, Hola, etc., while gathering the remaining millions into fortified concentration villages. So obnoxious were the colonial detention laws, regulations, and rules that their immediate abolition by the independent government was one of the top priorities in the 1961 Kenya African National Union (KANU) Manifesto:

Much of the current legislation denies the African people their rights and severely restricts their freedom. The Deportation of British Subjects Act has been invariably used to deny the African political and trade union leaders their freedom. Under this Act, the governor is empowered to make a deportation or a restriction order either in lieu of or in addition to the sentence imposed by a court of law against "undesirable persons." The Preservation of Public Security Ordinance (1959) and the Detained and Restricted Persons (Special Provisions) Ordinance (1959) are other legislation currently employed to detain Africans for eight years without trial. Not only are these leaders detained without trial but they are also detained under conditions which are inhuman. The restriction of our leaders at Lodwar, Lokitaung, Marsabit, Hola,

Manyani, suggests that, not only are they to suffer the deprivation of their liberty, but are deliberately confined to areas which are extremely hot, mosquito-ridden and deserted.

The KANU of 1961, as an instrument of Kenyan nationalism, was totally opposed to the sixty-year colonial culture of repressive violence and mass terror, so at independence in 1963, the Emergency Powers (Colonial Defence) Order in Council (1939) was repealed—although in reality the word "Emergency" was the only one deleted. As a spokesman for the new nationalist government explained, the word had, "for us the most distasteful associations of memory. . . . We prefer to talk about our public security."[3]

In fact, only the terminology changed. The Preservation of Public Security Act retained all the cardinal vices of the colonial detention laws—the unaccountability of the governor to the legislature, the waiving of the normal democratic assumption of a person's innocence until proven guilty, the provision that these regulations promulgated without the legislature are effective notwithstanding anything in the constitution or in any other law inconsistent therewith, and the assumption of a Kenyan's guilt for crimes of thought and intention.

By 1966 all the repressive colonial laws were back on the books. "Arise, Colonial Lazarus" was the neocolonials' celebratory call to divine worship at the holy shrines of imperialism:

Our father in Euromerican heaven,
Hallowed be thy name.
Thy Kingdom come.

Thy will be done
In our wealthy Africa now
As it was done in the colonial past.
Give us this day our daily dollar,
And forgive us our failures.
Help us triumph over those that challenge you
    and us,
And give us aid and the grace and the power to be
    meek and grateful
Forever and ever. Amen.

4

The Culture of Silence and Fear

1

Colonial Lazarus raised from the dead: this putrid specter of our recent history daily haunted us at Kamītī Prison. It hovered over us, its shadow looming larger and larger on our consciousness as days and nights rolled away without discernible end to our sufferings. We discussed its various shades and aspects, drawing on our personal experiences, often arriving at clashing interpretations and conclusions. Who raised colonial Lazarus from the dead to once again foul the fresh air of Kenya's dawn?

To a mistaken few, this was proof that human nature, white, black, or yellow, never changes; it remains evil. To others, it was a case of the mysterious biological nature of the ruling nationality, what they called tribe. Yet they could not explain how or why, apart from the Kenyan Somalis, the majority of the other prisoners came from the same community as some of those holding leadership in government. To a few, "Shauri ya Mungu tu" (It was merely an act of God), as Mzee Duale Roble Hussein used to put it during our walks on the prison-yard side-pavements. Yet to others, it was a case of civilian weakness and indiscipline: if only the military . . . ? For a few others, it was clear that this was one other result of the battle of classes and their interests, the fundamental feature behind all the vicissitudes of Kenyan history, more so after the European conquest and the establishment of colonial capitalism.

But we all shared a common feeling: something beautiful, something like the promise of a new dawn had been betrayed, and our presence and situation at Kamĩtĩ Maximum Security Prison was a logical outcome of that historical betrayal.

Irretrievable loss! Had we really come to this? Was prison our destiny as a Kenyan people? Fated always to plunge back to the days of the colony only hours after being tantalized with glimpses of new dawns? What of the million dead and maimed? Was it only to enable a depraved few to carry on the colonial philosophy for which the lives of countless poor men, women, and children had been sacrificed?

In the cell, each political prisoner would struggle against mounting despair—the inevitable outcome of bitter reflections churned over and over in the mind. For here one had no helper except one's own experiences and history. That, I would say, was the real loneliness of prison life. In the silence of one's cell, one had to fight, all alone, against a thousand demons struggling for the mastery of one's soul. Their dominant method was to show continually that there was only one way of looking at things, that there was only one history and culture, which moved in circles, so that the beginning and the end were the same. You moved only to find yourself back on the same spot. What was the point of making the effort? We were all the children of Sisyphus fated forever to roll the heavy stone of tyranny up the steep hill of struggle, only to see it roll back to the bottom.

But wait, I shouted back at the demons of despair. The African Sisyphus had another history, a beautiful history, a glorious history, and most Kenyan people were its best illustration. It is the history of a people ceaselessly struggling against feudal Arab slave dealers and against the Portuguese marauders who opened up Africa to her four hundred years of devastating European domination topped off by British predators embracing Kenya with bloody claws and fangs. Yes, it's the history of Kenyan people waging a protracted guerrilla war against a much better armed British imperialist power that used to boast of its invincibility to man and God. It's the history of Kenyan resistance culture, a revolutionary culture of courage and heroism, of the defiant Koitalel and Kĩmathi. It's a creative, fight-back culture unleashing tremendous energies among the Kenyan people.

Economically, this energy found its creative expression in the many industries set up by Kenyan people in times of national crisis. The Lumboko and Chetambe fortifications, built by the Bukusu people around Mount Elgon during their resistance against the British invasion of their country, still stand to this day as a living memorial to their courage and genius.

The KLFA set up underground clothing and armament industries in the cities and upon the mountains. People who only the other day were just carpenters, plumbers, and bicycle repairers now turned their skills into manufacturing pistols, rifles, and bombs under very difficult forest conditions. And they triumphed. The soldiers of the Kenya Land and Freedom Army broke the back of imperialism in Africa!

Politically, this energy found creative expression in the organizational efforts that enabled Koitalel to sustain a ten-year guerrilla struggle against vastly superior British might, a feat repeated by Kĩmathi in the 1950s. What is fascinating is how quickly the needs of the struggle compelled such leaders to see the imperative of greater unity among the various nationalities. Koitalel tried to forge a political alliance with the Luo and Baluhya peoples; Me Katilili's oath was an attempt to unify coastal nationalities and clans; and Kĩmathi attempted a grand political alliance of Kenyan people to oust the imperialist enemy.

In the arts, resistance energy found expression in songs, poems, plays, and dances, giving rise to a great progressive literary tradition of Kenyan poetry and theater. There was, for instance, the Ituĩka, a revolutionary cultural festival of music, dance, poetry, and theater among the Agĩkũyũ, which was enacted every twenty-five years, both as a ceremony transferring power from one generation to the other and as a communal renewal of commitment to struggle against tyrants as their forefathers, the Iregi[1] generation, had done.

During the 1930s, Mũthĩrĩgũ dances and songs made fun of the missionaries and voiced people's rejection of forced labor, their disgust with cultural imperialism, their uncompromising opposition to political oppression, and their strong condemnation of Kenyan collaborators with colonialist enemy occupation. The songs and dances were banned, and many Mũthĩrĩgũ artists were hounded to prison. But even behind prison bars, they went on singing their poetry of protest and commitment to freedom, ending with the chorus:

Gīthaka, Gīthaka gīkī
Gīthaka, Gīthaka gīkī
Twatigīirwo nī Iregi.

Land, this land
Land, this land
We inherited it from the revolutionaries.

The Mumboist anti-imperialist movement among the Luo and Gusii nationalities and the anti-imperialist religious movement called Dini ya Musambwa also gave rise to poetry and song, and many of the singers and composers were jailed or hounded to death. But they kept on creating new songs and new dances. Even the graphic artist Mabiro Kimolai of Sibou was arrested in 1913 when his silent art took up the cry of the people.

Finally, nearly the whole writing and publishing industry in the 1940s and 1950s supported the Kenya Land and Freedom Army. Volumes of songs, poems, and prose were published. Many more were simply committed to memory and were sung and recited in most homes or wherever two or more people had gathered. A people's theater flourished away from the stifling confines of walls, sets, and fixed stages.

Once again, the colonial overlords banned these publications; they banished the authors, composers, and publishers to concentration camps, prisons, and cruel deaths. But even behind the barbed wire and stone walls of the colonial Jericho, they went on composing new songs and singing out a collective defiance that finally brought those walls tumbling down:

> Tũtiũragia gũthamio
> Kana gũtwarwo Njera
> Kana gũtwarwo icigĩrĩra
> Tondũ tũtigatiga
> Gũtetera ithaka/Wĩyathi
> Kenya nĩ bũrũri wa andũ airũ.

> We are not afraid of detention
> Being sent to prison
> Banished to remote islands
> For we shall never give up
> Our struggle for Land/Freedom
> Kenya is an African people's country.

The period produced some romantic figures, like the legendary Maranga wa Gĩtonga, who would not leave his guitar behind as he went to fight in the forest.[2]

This culture generated courage, not fear; defiance of oppression, not submission; pride in self and in one's country, not cowardly acceptance of national humiliation; loyalty to Kenya, not its betrayal to imperialism. And it was precisely in reaction to the people's history of change and revolutionary culture that the colonial rulers had tried to humiliate Africa's Sisyphus into accepting the oppressor's view of history—that all efforts to change this reality would be futile.

Hardinge's philosophy of the sword and the bullet was a

reactionary response to the people's resistance against foreign occupation. Would Hardinge have called for bullets if there had been no armed resistance? Would he have tried to force submission if there had been no defiance? The Ituĩka revolutionary cultural festival and the Mũthĩrĩgũ dances and songs were suppressed because they lauded struggle to change an oppressive status quo. In their turn, the foreign missionary churches intensified efforts to promulgate colonial religions and cultures that glorified the beauty of accepting, even reveling in, one's own enslavement—to foreign gods and, by extension, to foreign masters, both of whom know what's best and only want to help you. After suppressing native people's own institutions of learning, like Gĩthũngũri Teachers' College and the Kikuyu Karĩng'a independent schools movement, which taught pride in self and country, the colonial regime built more church and government schools to propagate unchallenged the godly ideals of glory in submissive obedience.

Finally, the institution of British theater in Kenya in the 1950s was a reactionary response to the resurgence of popular dance and theater following the return of embittered Kenyan soldiers from the European-generated Second World War. The colonial regime had cause for alarm. The anti-imperialist Mũthuũ dances had spread in central Kenya like fire across a dry plain. In Nyeri, Kĩmathi had started the Gĩcamu theater movement with its base in Karũna-inĩ. Dance and theater had become a common feature in all of the people's own schools.

The British countered by starting theater clubs for British plays and players: the Little Theatre in Mombasa in 1948, the Donovan Maule Theatre in Nairobi in 1949, and similar clubs in Nakuru, Eldoret, and Kitale in the same period. In

1952 the colonial regime, in concert with the British Council, started the Kenya National Theatre. Here an annual schools' English drama festival was started, with the British Council as the main donor of prizes for deserving African children. During the same period, a European drama and music officer was appointed to control the growth of African theater in all Kenyan schools. In places like Alliance High School, the performance of Shakespeare became an annual ritual attended by colonial governors and applauding administrators.

In *Race Against Time*, Richard Frost,[3] former head of the Empire Information Service and the British Council's first representative in East Africa, offers fantastic revelations about the deliberate manner in which the whole imperialist cultural program was put into force. Frost writes that the Kenya National Theatre was built under direct instruction from the Colonial Office to meet the urgent need for fostering improved race relations through an organization which would aim, in the first place, at establishing primarily cultural facilities:

The National Theatre was built where it was because those who planned the scheme, including Thornly Dyer, the architect who designed the Parliament Building and conceived the master plan for Nairobi, wanted to build the National Theatre in the "snob" centre of Nairobi. The instruction given by the Secretary of State to the British Council Representative was to build a National Theatre and Cultural Centre where people of culture and position could meet. At that time no Africans were able to live anywhere near the site which was selected, but that site was chosen because it was hoped that in due time the residential apartheid would be brought to an end and Muthaiga, Westlands, the Hill and other areas, which were then open only to Europeans, would become districts where leading people of all races would live.

On the Kenya Drama Festival, Richard Frost is even more forthright about its being a cultural factory for manufacturing a multiracial Kenyan elite:

> The Kenya Drama Festival, which has an offshoot in the Schools Drama Festival, was the result of a plan put into operation in 1951. The British Council had to win the goodwill of Europeans and do what it could to help them to keep at a high standard the cultural heritage of Britain. Drama was a cultural activity enjoyed by both actors and audiences and it was also an activity in which Africans and Asians engaged. It was hoped that through the theatre the goodwill of the European community could be gained, European cultural standards could be helped, and, later on, members of the different races could be brought together by participation in a common pursuit which they all enjoyed.

Apart from schools, the Moral Re-Armament team toured concentration camps showing films with themes of wicked characters who find moral balance by rejecting the company of the wicked. At the same time, they tried to organize theater groups among the political prisoners to stage nice Christian plays about prodigal sons and forgiving fathers. They even recruited writers from among the political prisoners. In *Mau Mau Detainee*, J.M. Kariũki has described the emptiness of such theatre and writing:

> Benjamin was a very clever and able man and an expert at writing booklets in Kikuyu. He was a co-operator, but a most subtle one. He never beat anyone and he always treated the other political prisoners well. He composed a skilful pamphlet on "confession" which was given to us all. He also produced sketches and plays in which the man who had confessed was always richer or surpassed in some way the man who remained hardcore. The warders and the softcore liked these very much. We condemned them as the Wamarebe Plays.

Empty Tins Theatre: what an apt description of imperialist culture! Except that, unless countered, the cumulative effect of the repetition of the values of surrender can begin to make dents in the moral resolution of the recipients.

Kenyan people's theater survived this reactionary onslaught. In Nyeri, Theuri started a theater group on the ruins of those banned by the British. He staged plays in the Gĩkũyũ language. In schools like the Alliance High School, some students rebelled against the cult of Shakespeare and started writing their own plays in Kiswahili. They took them to the villages and locations around Nairobi and Nakuru, the heartland of settler culture. In the forests and the mountains, the Kenya Land and Freedom Army (Mau Mau) guerrillas continued their dances, songs, and theater with one main theme: death to British imperialism—and their black auxiliary army, the so-called Home Guards.

See now the dialectical workings of history: it was the British invaders who actually became terrified of the people's vigorous culture of revolutionary courage and optimistic determination. The indomitable strength and resilience of Kenyan popular culture had spread panic among the foreign settlers, who felt stalked by naked insecurity on every side. They now ate, drank, and even made love in their uniforms with newly sharpened bayonets and nailed boots. By the 1950s, in the high noon of their settler reactionary culture, their homes had become virtual fortifications, complete with ramparts, moats, spikes, sirens, and drawbridges, while bloodhounds, *mbwa kali*, kept guard at the gates of the erstwhile paradise.

Raise colonial Lazarus from the dead? The fact is that his heirs, the postcolonial ruling class, have also been caught in the dialectical net of history. Thus in Kenya today, the Kenya of colonial Lazarus resurrected, it is not the peasants and workers who walk about in abject terror. Why should they? They possess no stolen property to disturb their nightly sleep lest the owner should knock at the door. Their sole fear is that the police or the General Service Unit (GSU) will molest them.

On the contrary, it is the minority propertied class and its foreign friends who now walk the streets stalked by naked insecurity from every side. Their homes, like those of the settler minority whose culture they have chosen to emulate, have become virtual forts complete with guns, sirens, electronic surveillance, and bloodhounds, *mbwa kali*!

The neocolonial resurgence of this *mbwa kali* culture was

concretely demonstrated in 1979, when the guards of the American-owned Del Monte fruit company in Thika set their dogs on a couple of innocent Kenyan children, killing one girl and maiming the other. Their fear is such that they cannot even fully trust the coercive machinery of their state for total security. Might not that soldier or that police officer one day remember that he too is a worker of peasant origin, now earning a miserable Judas pay to suppress members of his own class? So they go for supplementary protection from foreigners. Foreign-owned security companies, like the London-based Securicor or the Israeli-run Ossica, are doing a lucrative business in Kenya as hired security officers in a vast ministry of fear. The *Weekly Review* of January 11, 1980 says:

> Good security is expensive, but the cost of no security is higher. Awareness of this fact has resulted in the proliferation of over 90 security firms throughout Kenya that employ no fewer than 20,000 people— as home guards, factory guards, guards for business premises and guards who escort cash in transit.
>
> Even though these firms might never be able to guarantee absolute security of property from theft, the call for guards grows. Home guards have even become a much-sought-after status symbol among affluent Kenyans. Not surprisingly many security firms tend to concentrate their home-guard services in Nairobi's posh residential areas to satisfy the high demand. But residents in a number of housing estates in the city also pool their resources to hire watchmen.

Securicor (Kenya) Limited is the biggest such organization. It was formed in 1969 when it acquired a
number of small local security firms complete with
staff and assets. In those days operations were confined
to Nairobi and Mombasa and the Securicor pay-roll
contained about 2,000 names. Today the company
employs more than 4,500 people and has 19 branches
in different parts of Kenya. . . . Securicor Kenya is part
of the British Securicor group, the largest industrial
security organization in Great Britain and one of the
biggest on the whole of the European continent.

Foreign-run private armies to protect foreigners and a handful
of Kenyans from real or imagined wrath of fellow Kenyans:
what an irony of history!

The culture of silence and fear had achieved a dialectically
opposite effect. Kenyan people had rejected the view of history
that the colonial and neocolonial gods had tried to impose on
rebellious Sisyphus. Why should I accept it?

2

In my cell, number 6, continuously thinking about the
beauty of our history, I became more and more convinced
that in their vindictive agitation for the banning of our theater efforts at Kamīrīthū and in their feverish clamor for my
incarceration, Kenya's rulers and their foreign friends had
been driven by fear. True to their colonial cultural inheri-
tance, they were mortally scared of peasants and workers who

showed no fear in their eyes and no submissiveness in their bearing, who proclaimed their history with unashamed pride and denounced its betrayal with courage. Yes, like their colonial counterparts, the rulers had become mortally afraid of the slightest manifestation of a people's outspoken culture of heroism and courage.

Eliud Njenga, the Kĩambu district commissioner who presided over the banning of the public performances of our play, *Ngaahika Ndeenda*, voiced the general panic of this class when, in an interview with the *Nairobi Times*, he claimed that on top of the play raising the best-be-forgotten issues of the nationalistic role of the soldiers of Kenya Land and Freedom Army, and the traitorous role of African members of the British Auxiliary Army (Home Guards) during the struggle for Kenya's independence, it was also calling for a class struggle.

He was, of course, wrong about the latter charge. The play, as afterward I tried to explain to the Detainee's Review Tribunal (chaired by a British ex-judge) of July 1978, could never have called into being what was already there. Classes and class struggle were the very essence of Kenyan history. The play didn't invent that history. It merely reflected it—correctly.

But the D.C. was expressing a deeper fear: the Kenyan ruling elite believed in the magic omnipotence of an imperialist colonial culture, but here were ordinary peasants and workers at Kamĩrĩthũ showing up the emptiness of borrowed culture and the potency of a people-based culture. Moreover, they were acting it out to thunderous applause from appreciative thousands who trekked on foot and in hired *matatu* and buses from all parts of the country. Was Kamĩrĩthũ becoming a revolutionary shrine?

3

Kamĩrĩthũ! It is difficult for me to conjure up in adequate literary terms the different images I have of Kamĩrĩthũ. The name is a diminutive form of Mĩrĩthũ, meaning a flat place on which rests a pool of water defiant to drought.[4] Little Mĩrĩthũ is bound by three sloping ridges that make it look like a rectangular trough, which is open on one of its smaller sides facing the Manguũ marshes. In my youth, all the sloping ridges were strips of cultivated fields with a few people's homesteads scattered about. A few Swahili *majengo*-tin-roofed type houses were built on the flat murram trough, away from the pool. It was a path through Kamĩrĩthũ that, starting in 1947, I followed daily to Kamandũra school, about two miles from home.

It was at Kamĩrĩthũ that I first saw Nyambura. I thought her the most beautiful woman I had ever seen, and I vowed then and there that she would one day be my wife. That this came to pass several years after I am sure had nothing to do with that boy's vow but everything to do with the fact that in the new Kamĩrĩthũ our two homes were separated by only a street, and I had not planned it. Njoki, my daughter whose photograph kept me company in prison, was named after Nyambura's mother, but the Kamĩrĩthũ peasants called the child Wamũingĩ, meaning that she belonged to them, she belonged to all Kamĩrĩthũ.

As part of Limuru, Kamĩrĩthũ is crucial to Kenya's history of struggle. Some Kikuyu Central Association (KCA) leaders, like Johana Wakĩraka, came from that area. The lands at Tigoni and Kanyawa, where in the 1920s people were ejected by force to make room for more European settlement, are only a few yards away from Kamĩrĩthũ. A railway line divided the stolen lands—where the settlers soon set up the Limuru Hunt, the Limuru Golf Course, the Limuru Racecourse, and the Limuru Farmers Corner, all high-class cultural rendezvous— from the African reservations, reservoirs of cheap labor and sex. I have tried to describe the landscape in *Weep Not, Child*, where Kipanga town stands for Limuru, or Rũngai, as the town was popularly known. One of the valleys described in *Weep Not, Child* originates from Kamĩrĩthũ.

When in 1948 I left the mission-run Kamandũra for the Gĩkũyũ Karĩng'a School at Manguũ, I never visited Kamĩrĩthũ except once briefly in 1953, when as a newly circumcised youth complete with my initiate's robe of white cloth decorated with several safety pins and one-cent pieces, I went across it, through the cultivated fields on one of the ridge slopes, and on to Tharũni and Ndeiya on the edges of Maasailand to visit other *rika* initiates to sing and dance the stick dance called *waine*.

That was in fact my very last impression of old Kamĩrĩthũ when in 1955 I went from my home village overlooking Limuru town to Alliance High School, Kikuyu, hidden in the guard-room of a goods train through the friendly efforts of Chris Kahara, then a railway official.[5] The year before, my elder brother, Wallace Mwangi wa Thiong'o, had joined the Kenya Land and Freedom Army (Mau Mau) after a dramatic escape from police custody. Many Home Guard loyalists would never forgive me for what some thought a miscarriage of educational justice: a brother of a Kenya Land and Freedom Army "terrorist" securing a place in one of the top African schools in colonial Kenya!

I came back after the first term and confidently walked back to my old village.[6] My home was now only a pile of dry mud-stones, bits of grass, charcoal, and ashes. Nothing remained, not even crops, except for a lone pear tree that slightly swayed in sun and wind. I stood there bewildered. Not only my home, but also the old village with its culture, its memories, and its warmth had been razed. Mwangi, who used to work for the Kahahu family next door, told me what had happened and pointed vaguely up the ridge. I walked up the ridge not knowing where I was headed until I met a solitary old woman. "Go to Kamīrīthū," she told me and pointed the way*.

Kamīrīthū was now no longer the name of a trough with a defiant pool of water surrounded by a few Swahili houses, but instead the name of a new "emergency village" on one of the sloping ridges next to the path I used to follow on my way to Kamandūra. I walked through the new village asking people for my new home and passed through the present site of Kamīrīthū Community Theatre. All around me, I saw women and children on rooftops with hammers and nails and poles and thatch, building the new homes because their men were in concentration camps or away with the people's guerrilla army. Many critics have noted the dominance of the theme of return in my novels, plays, and short stories, particularly in *A Grain of Wheat*. But none has known the origins of the emotion behind the theme. It is deeply rooted in my return to Kamīrīthū in 1955. The return of Kenya Land and Freedom Army political prisoners was to come later.

Initially, the village was a riotous mass of smoking straw-topped mushrooms. Later, in 1956 or 1957, when the decision was taken to turn the emergency concentration

---

*See my memoir, *In the House of the Interpreter*.

villages into permanent features to facilitate the creation of an African landed middle class through land consolidation and the enclosure system, while retaining the villages as permanent reservoirs of cheap labor for both the whites' highlands and the new African landlords, the village was expanded with slightly better planning. The yeomen were later allowed to build homes in their enclosures, and they quit the villages. The landless remained. Four acres of land were set aside for a youth center. A mud-walled barracks-type building was put up there. That was all.

Kamĩrĩthũ has not changed much from its emergency origins. Poverty is still the king. Many families live in shacks beside the village paths. And of course Kamĩrĩthũ is still a reservoir of cheap labor for the new Kenyan landlords and the Euro-American multinationals who at independence replaced the former British landlords in the sprawling green fields of tea and coffee around Tigoni and beyond. To be wealthy in Kenya today is incomplete without land in Limuru. The golf course and the racecourse remain. The Limuru Hunt is still the big event of the year. Every weekend, a troupe of unemployed youth from Kamĩrĩthũ go to the Tigoni Golf Club to offer their services as caddies for the local and foreign golf-playing tycoons.

During the Emergency, the youth center at Kamĩrĩthũ was the meeting place for boys and girls to dance *erithi* and *nyangwĩcũ* and other dances of the period. After independence, the center came under the Limuru Area Council, and a few carpentry classes were started. In 1974, the Limuru Area Council was disbanded. The center had now nobody to look after it. But it remained, a four-classroom barracks with broken walls, occupying about a quarter of an acre, the other four and three-quarters making a grazing ground for a few lonely cows and goats. The village children also found the site a good common ground for wrestling and throwing dice. They also used it for craps in a different sense—as a toilet—and the stench was overpowering. There has never been any health program for this village of more than ten thousand souls.

The only major cultural activity on this grass in Kamĩrĩthũ occurred in 1976 when the University of Nairobi Free Travelling Theatre, run by the Department of Literature, performed some plays, including extracts from *The Trial of Dedan Kimathi*, written by Mĩcere Mũgo and me. Otherwise the center was dead to organized performance culture.

It was through the tireless efforts of a community development officer, Njeri wa Amoni, that a new committee made up of concerned villagers was formed to revive the center and run it on a self-help basis. That was how I came to join the new management committee under the chairmanship of Adolf Kamau, a peasant farmer, and later Ngigĩ Mwaũra, then a sales director with a motor vehicle company.[7] Karanja, a primary-school teacher from the village, was the secretary. But the majority of the committee members were peasants and workers from the village.

The committee changed the name of the youth center to Kamĩrĩthũ Community Education and Cultural Centre, reflecting a new ambitious program for uplifting the place and changing the lives of the villagers through what we called a *harambee* of sweat. The committee decided that money was not the basis of development. Human hands and brains were the basis. Cooperative labor, not money and *harambee* charity handouts, was going to develop the center along several broad lines and phases: adult education (adult literacy, continuing education, etc.), cultural development (music, dance, drama, etc.), material culture (furniture, basketry, leatherwork, music crafts—the making of all the material objects daily used by the community), and health. The center was going to be run on a democratic collective decision-making basis, all of us drawing on our different experiences in identifying and tackling problems. Each problem area would have a subcommittee. Initially, two subcommittees were set up, for education and culture, with provision for two more to deal with community health and material culture.

I was elected the chairman of the cultural committee, and Ngũgĩ wa Mĩriĩ, a researcher in adult literacy at the University of Nairobi, the chairman of the education committee. The first program was literacy; the center started with a class of fifty-five workers and peasants in June 1976, and by the end of the year, all could read and write in Gĩkũyũ language. We had established roots.

We were now ready to venture into cultural activities. Here most of the peasants and workers were quite clear as to what they wanted. Some had already participated in or seen concerts and playlets by a group of workers at Saint Lwanga Catholic Church at Kamĩrĩthũ. Others had seen the plays of the University of Nairobi Free Travelling Theatre. Yet others had been to the controversial Kenya National Theatre in Nairobi in October 1976 and had seen the Kenya Festac '77 Drama Group's performance of the complete version of *The Trial of Dedan Kimathi* as brilliantly directed by Seth Adagala. Now they wanted similar efforts at Kamĩrĩthũ!

Plays would serve three main purposes. They would serve as entertainment and collective self-education; they would serve as follow-up reading material for the new literates; and they would raise money to finance the other programs and meet the day-to-day expenses like chalk, writing materials, and electricity bills.

That was how in December 1976 Ngũgĩ wa Mĩriĩ and I came to be given the task of producing a working script. The script had to be ready by March 1977.

We couldn't meet the March deadline. But by April 1977, an outline of the script of *Ngaahika Ndeenda* was ready. For the next two months, the peasants added to the script, altering this and that. Reading of the final working script and rehearsals started on June 5, 1977. The performances commenced on October 2, the twenty-fifth anniversary of the declaration of the State of Emergency and the beginning of the Kenya Land and Freedom Army's armed struggle.

The six months between June and November 1977 were the most exciting in my life and the true beginning of my education. I learned my language anew. I rediscovered the creative nature and power of collective work.

Work, oh yes, work! Work, from each according to his ability for a collective vision, was the great democratic equalizer. Not money, not book education, but work. Not three-piece suits with carnations and gloves, not tongues of honey, but work. Not birth, not palaces, but work. Not globetrotting, not the knowledge of foreign tongues and foreign lands, not dinners at foreign Inns of Court, but work. Not religions, not good intentions, but work. Work and yet more work, with collective democratic decisions on the basis of frank criticisms and self-criticism, was the organizing principle, which gradually became the cornerstone of our activities.

Although the overall direction of the play was under Kĩmani Gecau, the whole project became a collective community effort as peasants and workers took more and more initiative in revising and adding to the script, in directing dance movements on the stage, and in the general organization.

I saw with my own eyes an incredible discipline emerge in keeping time and in cutting down negative social practices. Drinking alcohol, for instance. It was the women's group, led by Gaceri wa Waiganjo, who imposed on themselves a ban on drinking alcohol, even a glass, when coming to work at the center. This spread to all the other groups, including the audience. By the time we came to perform, it was generally understood and accepted that drunkenness was not allowed at the center. For a village known for drunken brawls, it was a remarkable achievement of collective self-discipline that we never had a single incident of fighting or a single drunken disruption for all the six months of public rehearsals and performances.

I saw with my own eyes peasants, some of whom had never once been inside a theater in their lives, design and construct an open-air theater complete with a raised stage, roofed dressing rooms and storerooms, and an auditorium with a seating capacity of more than two thousand persons. Under a production team led by Gatonye wa Mũgoiyo, an office messenger, they experimented with matchsticks on the ground before building a small working model on which they based the final complex.

The rehearsals, arranged to fit in with the working rhythms of the village, which meant mostly Saturday and Sunday after-

noons, were all in the open, attracting an ever increasing crowd of spectators and an equally great volume of running appreciative or critical commentaries. The whole process of play acting and production had been demystified, and the actors and the show were the gainers for it. The dress rehearsal on Sunday, September 25, 1977, attracted one of the biggest crowds I have ever seen for a similar occasion, and the same level of high attendance was maintained for the next four Saturdays and six Sundays.

The effort unleashed a torrent of talents hitherto unsuspected even by the owners. Thus before the play was over, we had already received three scripts of plays in the Gĩkũyũ language, two written by a worker, and one by a primary-school teacher. One unemployed youth, who had tried to commit suicide four times because he thought his life was useless, now suddenly discovered that he had a tremendous voice, which, when raised in a song, kept its listeners on dramatic tenterhooks. None of the actors had ever been on a stage before, yet they kept the audiences glued to their seats, even when it was raining.

One of the most insulting compliments came from a critic who wrote that the orchestra was professional and had been hired from Nairobi. Another such compliment came from those who heatedly argued that simple villagers could never attain that level of excellence, that the actors were all university students dressed in the tattered clothes of peasants. Another equally insulting compliment came from a university lecturer in literature who argued that the apparent effortless ease of the acting was spontaneous: after all, the villagers were acting themselves. The fact was that all the actors and musicians, men, women and children, came from the village, and they put in more than four months of conscious disciplined work. Some of our university lecturers and those other critics, in their petit bourgeois blindness, simply couldn't conceive of peasants as being capable of sustained, disciplined intellectual efforts.

As for me, I learned a lot. I had been relegated to the role of a messenger and a porter, running errands here and there. But I also had time to observe things. I saw how the people had appropriated the text, improving on the language and episodes and metaphors, so that the play, which was finally put on to a fee-paying audience on Sunday, October 2, 1977, was a far cry from the original tentative awkward efforts that Ngũgĩ and I had put together. I felt one with the people. I shared their rediscovery of their collective strength and abilities, and their joyous feeling that they could accomplish anything—even transform the whole village and their lives without a single *harambee* of charity—and I could feel the way the actors were communicating their joyous sense of a new power to their audiences, who went home with gladdened hearts.

Before long, we had received one delegation from Gĩkambura village, in Kikuyu, and another from Kanyarĩrĩ, asking how they too could start a similar community cultural project. A group of teachers came from Nyandarwa North, and they too wanted to start their own Kamĩrĩthũ.

Then suddenly the KANU government, through its Kĩambu district commissioner, struck with venom. In a letter to the chairman of Kamĩrĩthũ Community Educational and Cultural Centre dated December 16, 1977, he withdrew the license for further performances of *Ngaahika Ndeenda*, plunging a three-year-old communal vision into a sea of sorrow and depression. He later gave reasons for banning further performances, citing public security. He should have more truthfully cited the public insecurity of a few individuals who thought their reservoir of cheap labor and sex was threatened by the new confidence generated among the villagers by the new theater.

The comprador bourgeoisie could have their golf, polo, cricket, rugby, tennis, squash, and badminton, their horse and motor races, their royal hunts, their German, American, French, English, and Italian theater, cinema, music, and concerts, their swimming pools and expensive sauna and massage clubs, their choice of expensive drinks after an easy day's work, their gambling casinos and striptease joints with imported white nudes, and their endless cocktail parties with participants featured in the socialite pages of *Viva*, the *Daily Nation*, and *Chic*, but peasants with clods of clay had no right to a theater that correctly reflected their lives, fears, hopes, dreams, and history of struggle, had no right to their own creative efforts even in their own backyards. The church, with its eternal call for submissive trust and blind obedience, and the foreign-owned breweries of mass-produced soporific drinks were now their only legal cultural alternatives.

These men who had so callously razed the Kamĩrĩthũ people's cultural effort to the ground (some, like the D.C. Kĩambu, had not even bothered to see it) had acted in the dog-in-the-manger tradition of those "faceless faces of important men" once described by Sylvia Plath in her poem "Three Women":

> It is these men I mind:
> They are so jealous of anything that is not flat! They
>   are jealous gods
> That would have the whole world flat because
>   they are.

They might be flat, but they had the power of police truncheons and law courts, of the bullet and the prison, and woe unto them who challenge the legal enforcement of flatness!

A problem remained, however. The office of the district commissioner, Kĩambu, had duly licensed the play's performances. Everything at the center had been done in the open, including the play-reading sessions, the selection of actors, and all the rehearsals. Kamĩrĩthũ Community Education and Cultural Centre was itself legally registered as a self-help project with the Department of Community Development of the Ministry of Housing and Social Services.

In its official submissions to the UNESCO general assembly in Nairobi in 1976, the government had made a very strong case for rural development integrated with culture, including rural village theaters as a central core of the program, and this proposal had been accepted. Indeed, a senior cabinet minister in the government was then the current president of UNESCO. Now a popular people's play had been refused further performances by a government that had hosted UNESCO and endorsed its cultural policies, and no satisfactory reason was forthcoming!

How now to deceive the nation and the whole world? Incarcerate the whole village? Detain a whole community? But there had been no riots, no drunken brawls, and no open defiance of any existing laws. On the contrary, the crime rate and drunkenness in the village had markedly fallen for the duration of the play's run! Besides, detaining a whole village would severely drain a necessary reservoir of cheap labor. Who would now pick tea leaves and coffee beans? Who would cultivate the fields for a pittance?

For them, there was an easier way. What right had a university professor to work with ragged-trousered workers and tattered peasants and even "pretend" to be learning from a people whose minds we have decreed should never rise above the clods of clay they daily break? What is he really up to? Let us thwart his intentions—whatever they are. Incarcerate the clever fellow!

And they did! At midnight, December 30, 1977, they took me from my home and led me to Kamītī Maximum Security Prison in chains. For a whole year, I was to remain in cell 16 wrestling with multifarious demons in the dry wilderness of Kamĩtĩ Prison, contemplating the two dialectically opposed traditions of Kenyan history and culture and colonial aesthetics. They had raised colonial Lazarus from the dead. Who will bury him again?

5

Wrestling with Colonial Demons

1

Wrestling with demons in the stony and dusty wilderness of Kenya's detention camps since 1895 has produced two types of political prisoners: those who finally succumbed and said yes to an oppressive system and those who defied and said "Never!"

The demons led the acquiescent types down the abyss of despair to a valley of white bones. There they allowed them a glimpse of African Sisyphus endlessly laboring to push up the rock of oppression, only to see it roll back to the original spot. This is your black fate, the demons told them, and waited for their reactions. When the demons saw that they believed this vision of despair, they let it overwhelm the prisoner. Then sympathetically and graciously they would offer mediation services. First they would give the prisoner another dose of pessimism. The prisoners sank further into despair; they felt helpless. Then suddenly or gradually, depending on how they read their character and the situation outside the stony wilderness, the demons showed them the only way to personal salvation: "See no evil. Hear no evil. Resist not evil." The prisoner who took that way out came out of the wrestling match a broken soul, ready to denounce in words and deeds his previous stands and actions.

Harry Thuku was the greatest threat to colonial settlerdom in the 1920s. As the leader of the East African Association, he inspired the workers to organize to fight against forced labor, female and child slavery, high taxation without even a little representation, low wages, and the oppressive *kipande* (identity paper) that all African males sixteen or older were obliged to carry chained around their necks. Unlike some labor leaders, who bought into the view that trade unionism could be divorced from politics, Harry Thuku clearly saw that the solution to the workers' problems lay in politics. The economic emancipation of the worker would come through political struggle and never through apolitical trade unionism.

Thus the East African Association further demanded that Kenya must not be a colony, that elections to the legislative council should be on a common roll, and that all the stolen lands should be returned to the rightful owners. Harry Thuku strenuously fought and exposed the divisive ideology of racism, rejecting, for instance, the white settlers' attempts to divide Asian and African workers. This was the Harry Thuku[1] who could write so movingly about the emerging unity of workers of different nationalities and religious faiths. He wrote in the workers' newspaper *Tangazo*:

I was very delighted to be travelling to the meeting at Ng'enda because I was accompanied by the

school-teacher, Samuel Okoth, a Christian from
Maseno; and two Muslims, their names were Abdulla
Tairara and Ali Kironjo. We were very pleased at our
trip for we travelled as brothers. And I saw no difference between the Kavirondo and the man from
Kikuyu, or even between the Christian believer and
the believer in Islam.

Thus, the famed "traditional rivalry" between Agĩkũyũ and
the Luo people was clearly a later colonial invention. The fact
is that, right from the beginning, the two nationalities had
the biggest working-class elements. Unity among Mũgĩkũyũ
workers and Jaluo workers (because of their numbers) was
always a threat to imperialism in Kenya, and Harry Thuku
understood this. Unfortunately, so did the settlers and the
long line of Kenyan collaborators with imperialism. They had
to create artificial rivalry, as they still do.

This was the Harry Thuku who, on being threatened by the
colonial regime with the choice of either losing his well-paid
job at the treasury or giving up political struggle, promptly and
proudly replied, "I choose politics." This was indeed the Harry
Thuku who could see that colonial chiefs, like Kĩnyanjui, were
like dogs: "They bark at the sound of other dogs, when their
masters want them to, and also when they want to be fed by
the government."

Not surprisingly, his arrest on March 14, 1922, brought about
one of the biggest workers' mass protests and demonstrations
ever in the streets of Nairobi. The colonial regime, true to its
cultural traditions, responded to the workers' demands for

Thuku's release with mounted troops and rifles. One hundred fifty workers, including their leader, Mary Mũthoni Nyanjirũ, were massacred. At the Norfolk Hotel, the "House of Lords," the settlers—the Happy Valley crowd—joined in the massacre and cheered and drank whisky at the sight of the workers' blood. This Harry Thuku has already moved into the realm of legend, and I have treated him as such in the early chapters of my novel *A Grain of Wheat.*

After nine years of lonely detention and imprisonment at Kismayu, Lamu, and Marsabit, where he was constantly indoctrinated by the demons in the physical form of district commissioners, he came back, joined the militant KCA (the political successor to his banned East African Association) and he, having succumbed, immediately tried to turn it into a colonial instrument.

Fortunately, Jesse Kariũki and the other KCA leaders saw through him. This was a different Thuku from the one for whom women workers had composed a praise song, nicknaming him Mũnene wa Nyacĩng'a. In people's politics, there is no room for sentimentality. It can prove fatal and treacherous to a movement, and the KCA leaders had grasped this. They threw him out.

Harry Thuku wasted no time in acting out his new chosen role of colonial messenger. He formed a loyalist Kikuyu Provincial Association to fight against the Kenya nationalists:

Every member of this organization will be pledged to be loyal to His Majesty the King of Great Britain and the established government and will be bound to do nothing which is not constitutional according to the British traditions or do anything which is calculated to disturb the peace, good order or government.

This colonial zombie, a total negation of his earlier predetention self, could years later write admiringly about colonial chiefs whom earlier he had correctly described as dogs:

> Some of the bravest people during Mau Mau were the Christians; many were murdered because they refused to take the oath. And if they were forced they would go and confess the next day. Chief Njiiri was like this too. When the Emergency broke out, he hoisted the Union Jack in the centre of his village, and I remember one meeting with Sir Evelyn Baring where I was present when Njiiri asked for permission to go into the forest and fight "these evil people" himself.

He should have added that the same chief was later to smash his radio set to pieces when in 1961 he heard that Kenyatta and the other nationalist leaders were to be released from prison to return home to lead Kenya into independence.

In his autobiography, published in 1970, Harry Thuku shows not the slightest awareness of his divided loyalties. The colonial ethic of submissive trust had done its work. Harry Thuku was broken by nine years of detention and imprisonment and said yes to colonial culture.

Jomo Kenyatta was another terror of colonial settlerdom and imperialism in the 1930s and 1950s. This was the Kenyatta who, as a KCA delegate in London, wrote in the *Sunday Worker* of October 27, 1929, words still ringing with contemporary relevance in today's anti-imperialist struggles:

> The present situation means that once again the natives of the colony are showing their determination not to submit to the outrageous tyranny which has been their lot since the British robbers stole their land. . . . [Kenyans] have found themselves constantly denuded of their land, and compelled by means of forced labour to work the vast natural wealth of their country for the profit of their interloping imperialist bosses. Discontent has always been rife among [Kenyans] and will be so until they govern themselves. . . . Sir Edward Grigg talks of "agitation"; there is agitation, an agitation that meets a hearty response from robbed and maltreated Africans, and will not cease until we are our own rulers again.[2]

Recalling the 1922 massacre of Kenyan workers outside the Norfolk Hotel, he wrote a strong denunciation in the *Daily Worker* of January 1930 with the prophetic words that Kenyan people will never forget these imperialist atrocities:

> I was in the crowd myself and saw men, women and children killed, and many others lying in agony. It was a most terrible massacre of people who were quite unarmed and defenceless, and the people of Kenya will not forget.

Or later in 1934, in his contribution to Nancy Cunard's anthology, *Negro*:

> Kenya is the most important British colony in East Africa. . . . During the past thirty-five years [our] people have been robbed of their best land and are reduced to the status of serfs forced to work on their own lands for the benefit of the white "owners," and even in some circumstances to work without pay or food. . . . The soul of the African is stricken nigh to death by confiscation of its ancestral lands, the obstruction of its free development in social and economic matters, and its subjugation to an imperialist system of slavery, tax-paying, pass-carrying, and forced labour. This policy of British imperialist robbery and oppression aroused the greatest alarm and anxiety amongst the Kenyan Africans, the outcome of which was the revolt of 1922, when defenceless Africans, men, women and children, were shot down by these filibusters.

Yes, this was the Kenyatta who could castigate in the strongest possible terms the colonial Happy Valley culture of golf, polo, whisky, whoredom, and murder of Africans for sport. He condemned the seduction of African girls "to satisfy their bestial lust," concluding that colonialist "civilization is all in the interest of capitalist greed and imperialist exploitation." In the 1933 issue of Marcus Garvey's *Negro Worker*, he wrote, "The missionaries . . . are agents of the imperialists who teach Africans that they must tolerate all oppression and exploitation in order that they shall have a good home and better conditions in heaven when they die."

In the November 1933 issue of the *Labour Monthly*, Kenyatta might almost have been talking about the Africa of the 1980s when he wrote the following prophecy:

Perhaps many will ask: what can we do against an imperialist government which is armed with machine guns, aeroplanes and guns, etc? My answer to that is we have learnt examples from other countries. And the only way out is the mass organization of workers and peasants of various tribes, and by having this unity we shall be in a position to put up a strong protest against this robbery and exploitation.

There, all Kenyan Africans must fight for their liberation. We cannot forget how we have been exploited and oppressed through these solemn "pledges." Let none of our countrymen have any faith in these imperialist hypocritical "promises" which mean nothing but the oppression and exploitation of the masses. In this fight we shall have the support of all who are oppressed by the British slave empire—the Indians, the Irish, the South Africans—all these people are revolting against this damnable empire whose days are numbered.

With the support of all revolutionary workers and peasants we must redouble our efforts to break the bonds that bind us. We must refuse to give any support to the British imperialists either by paying taxes or obeying any of their slave laws! We can fight in

unity with the workers and toilers of the whole world,
and for a free Africa.

Good morning, revolution! The Kenyatta of the 1930s was
talking about the imminent inevitable collapse of the old British Empire, falling to the united blows of its enslaved workers and peasants. Yes, Kenyatta was talking about a liberated
Kenya, concretely meaning the liberation of all the workers
and peasants of all the Kenyan nationalities from imperialist
economic exploitation and political and cultural oppression.
More, he was talking of a free Africa—in 1933!

This was the Kenyatta of "the burning spear," of whom the
Kenyan masses then rightly sang as their coming savior. This
was the Kenyatta reflected in my novel *Weep Not, Child*, about
whom the peasant characters whispered at night. The remnant
of this Kenyatta could still, in 1952 at the Kapenguria trial,
denounce imperialist justice and reject any and every abject
accommodation.

In saying this, I am asking for no mercy at all on behalf
of my colleagues. We are asking that justice may be
done and that the injustices that exist may be righted.

Following the tone he set, the rest of the Kapenguria Six stood
luminously splendid in their defiant rejection of imperialist
justice: "Impose any sentence you like!" they all said, and they
were jailed.

What happened to that Kenyatta during the ten years of
prison life in lonely, dusty places? In the prisons, reading
only the Bible and the Koran, with the district commissioner

constantly calling him to private audiences away from the other four, did the demons, in the ghostly forms of Ross, Hooper, Barlow, and Arthur—all the early missionaries who used to write to him in the 1930s urging him to return to church fellowship and give up "extreme" politics—did these now visit him and, raising him from the valley of dry bones, showed him the escape route from the ceaseless, fruitless labors of African Sisyphus? Did they then take him to the mountaintop and show him all the personal glory accruing to him who would kneel before the God of imperialism and offer prayers of devotion?—to be sprinkled of course, with occasional nationalist slogans borrowed from past memories.

Evidence of such visitations now comes from the work of a die-hard settler. Michael Blundell was the leader of the settlers and a leading architect of ways and means of suppressing Kenya Land and Freedom Army (Mau Mau) and African nationalism. In his settler memoirs, *So Rough a Wind*, he describes a secret visit to Kenyatta in detention:

> We had a long talk together, especially on the land problems of the poorer Kikuyu, with which he had always been so concerned. When I was leaving to get into my car, he asked me why the Europeans disliked him so much. I thought it best to tell him the truth; that they associated him with the evil side of Mau Mau and considered that he had planned and initiated the movement, with all its horrors and murders; and felt that he hated them and would not treat them fairly if he ever achieved power. He asked me what he should do as this was a wrong analysis of his feelings,

although he was determined that Africans were the leaders and first-class citizens in their own country. I replied that I could not help him, that I firmly believed the new African world needed the best of the Europeans and that only he could correct, by his speeches and actions, the impressions which many Europeans sincerely held about him. He took no offence at this straightforward talk, but nodded his head, grunting away the while, which is a habit of his when considering anything.

Did Kenyatta enter into some secret agreement with the British while he was in detention? Or did he merely act on the advice of the likes of Michael Blundell?

At any rate, the Kenyatta who came out of detention and imprisonment in 1961 was talking an entirely different language from the one he used to speak when he was "the burning spear" of nationalistic politics. The new Kenyatta now went to Nakuru, the heartland of white colonial settlerdom, on August 12, 1963, soon after the KANU victory, and he actually asked the erstwhile imperialist murderers and sadists to forgive him for whatever wrongs he had done them, just as Blundell had asked him to do:

> If I have done wrong to you it is for you to forgive me. If you have done wrong to me, it is for me to forgive you. . . . We want you to stay and farm this country.

But to the Kenyan workers and peasants and the stalwarts of the Kenya Land and Freedom Army (Mau Mau), he was talking a language of threats almost as if they were now his main enemies. Indeed his assurances to the settlers and imperialist foreigners about their special protected role in an independent Kenya was a slap in the face to the many Kenyans who had fought precisely to get imperialists off the back of Kenya's economy:

> The government of an independent Kenya will not be a gangster government. Those who have been panicky about their property—whether land or buildings or houses—can now rest assured that the future African government will not deprive them of their property or rights of ownership.

As Bishop Abel Muzorewa was later to do in Zimbabwe, this new Kenyatta, now preaching "forgive and forget and follow me," sent the army inherited from colonial times to hunt down the remaining guerrillas, describing them as "these evil men, vagrants."

This action was of course quite consistent with the anti-Kenya Land and Freedom Army (Mau Mau) denunciatory line he had taken in 1952 and at Kapenguria: "The government, instead of joining with us to fight Mau Mau, they arrested all the leading members of KAU (Kenya African Union)." What was surprising was the ready swiftness with which he went about eliminating the fighters. It is interesting that throughout his life as prime minister and president of an independent Kenya, he never allowed the remains of Kĩmathi to be removed from Kamĩtĩ Prison to a symbolic shrine of honor. It is interesting too that Kenyatta never allowed a single former militant associate of KAU and KLFA of predetention days near the seats of power.

This deliberate and conscious effort to remove Kenya Land and Freedom Army and other nationalistic elements from the central stage of Kenyan politics always reached ridiculous heights during the commemorative month of October, in which Kenyatta was usually spoken of as the sole fighter, the man who singlehandedly won Kenya's independence. It was as if such others as Kaggia, Oneko, and the millions of dead and detained had been wiped off the face of known and written history.

For administration and for political advice, the new Kenyatta relied more and more on those who used to be actively anti-KLFA, or on colonial chiefs and sons of colonial chiefs. The sole remaining symbol of KLFA militancy to occupy a place of national importance after independence was J.M. Kariūki. He too was murdered in 1975.

In Kenyatta's officially collected speeches, *Harambee*, all his old anti-colonial, anti-imperialist, anti-exploitation, and anti-oppression statements and articles were deliberately excluded. Indeed, the new Kenyatta, like Harry Thuku before him, could now only cite personal accumulation as the sole criterion of one's moral and political worth. The ethics of serve-self-first are clearly articulated in his now famous attack on Bildad Kaggia, at Kandara, on April 11, 1965, only a year and five months after independence:

> We were together with Paul Ngei in jail. If you go to Ngei's home, he has planted a lot of coffee and other crops. What have you done for yourself? If you go to

[Fred] Kubai's home, he has a big house and has a nice shamba [plantation]. Kaggia, what have you done for yourself? We were together with Kũng'ũ Karũmba in jail, now he is running his own buses. What have you done for yourself?

Here independence was interpreted as a golden opportunity for personal gain. Anyone who didn't grab was lazy. In fact there has now grown up a clan of Kenyans who, following the colonial tradition of European settlers, pride themselves on their hard work and efficiency. But this "hard work and efficiency" consists of pocketing a small commission fee for every 10 million shillings they let go out of the country on the shoulders of foreign investments. Seen in terms of grabbing wealth, then the European settlers had been a most efficient and hard-working lot, for they had gone about it day and night, from 1895 to 1963. It is interesting that in his Kandara attack on radical nationalism, the point of departure or reference is not KCA or KAU or Kenya Land and Freedom Army (Mau Mau) but prison. It was as if Kaggia had broken some collective resolution agreed to in detention!

Because of his revolutionary KCA-influenced past, his pan-African associations with Kwame Nkrumah, C.L.R. James, Paul Robeson, George Padmore, and W.E.B. Du Bois, his KAU nationalistic phase, the cult of revolutionary anti-imperialist personality built around him while he was in prison, and his consummate, almost instinctive sense of political opportunism, the new Kenyatta went on fooling his peasant admirers, who always thought that he still concealed, behind his gold-dyed beard and hypnotic eyes, a master plan for Kenya's final deliverance from external and internal exploitation. "Our Kenyatta knows what he's doing" was the general ambiguous attitude even when they felt uneasy about the influx of imperialist Europeans in an independent Kenya. Of course, they were right. Kenyatta was too much of a political opportunist not to know what he was doing. But for most Kenyans, the truth that this was not the Kenyatta of progressive Kenyan nationalism came to light with the callous, brutal murder of J.M. Kariũki and the subsequent official cover-up. This Kenyatta had finally said yes to the colonial culture of fear at Lodwar, Lokitaung, and Maralal.

In the novel *A Grain of Wheat*, I tried, through Mũgo, who carried the burden of mistaken revolutionary heroism, to hint at the possibilities of the new Kenyatta. But that was in 1967, and nothing was clear then about the extent to which Kenyatta had negated his past, nor the sheer magnitude of the suffering it would cause to our society today.

2

The negation of a previous progressive position by the type of political prisoner exemplified by Thuku and Kenyatta cannot entirely be attributed to their lonely wrestles during imprisonment with the demons of surrender. In the case of both Thuku and Kenyatta, the roots of their political about-face lay in their petit bourgeois[3] class positions (the result of missionary education), which they never quite transcended by fully and consciously immersing themselves in the fortunes of the peasantry and working class. Kenyatta was always torn between the power and might of imperialism and the power and might of the masses. He was therefore strong or weak depending on which individuals or groups were closest to him, pro-imperialist, or anti-imperialist.

He was very strong in the 1930s when he was close to the Kikuyu Central Association (KCA) and other radical nationalists, and later when he was in England with radical pan-Africanists like C.L.R. James, Paul Robeson, W.E.B. Du Bois, and Kwame Nkrumah, leading to his participation in the 1945 Fifth Pan-African Congress. But toward the end of the 1930s, he had lost touch with Kenyan-based anti-imperialist nationalist organizations, and two people—Professor Bronisław Malinowski and Mbiyũ Koinange—had come into his life reinforcing the reactionary tendencies of his own class. Professor Malinowski led him down the easy paths of cultural nationalism through a study of anthropology, which culminated in the publication of Kenyatta's *Facing Mount Kenya*, with its obvious attempts to hold back the political bitterness that progressive Africans necessarily felt then. Nevertheless, Kenyatta's previous KCA-influenced radical anti-imperialism was strong enough to leave a mark on the general political tone of *Facing Mount Kenya*. The seminal study and the resolutions of the Fifth Pan-African Congress were still ringing in his ears when finally he returned to Kenya in 1946.

Mbiyũ Koinange has never really condemned imperialism. His politics have never gone beyond the call for an end to the color bar in acquiring land, in the holding of public office, and in social life. He remained the educated son of an enlightened chief, but with a strong admiration for mystical feudalism. In 1933, Mbiyũ was defending British colonialism in Kenya:

It is an undeniable fact that the natives of Africa have benefited by British administration, for, regardless of its failures in some respects, the British Government has shown a desire for fair play in its dealings with the Natives.

This was at a time when even his own father was demanding the return of the stolen lands, and Kenyatta was calling for the violent overthrow of British imperialism not only in Kenya but also in the whole of Africa. The decisive intervention of the university-educated Mbiyū in the life of the virtually self-educated Kenyatta at certain strategic moments in 1938, 1946, and 1963, has been disastrous for Kenya's nationalism and modern history.

In the only book that he has published, *The People of Kenya Speak for Themselves* (1955), Mbiyū was at pains to prove the blessings of multi-racialism if only the color bar would end in Kenya. This may not have been surprising in the 1950s. What is surprising is that in 1979, he allowed a reprint of the book. On page 75 of the reprint appears the following: "The Kenyan people, without settler domination, would be of infinitely more value and service to the British Commonwealth of Nations than all the mess settlers have created both in Kenya and in the eyes of the world. The people of Kenya, free from settler domination, would make a powerful contribution to the British people."[4]

For Thuku, similar interventions came in the form of selected friendly priests and "objective" colonial district administrators who called on him to give advice on the basis of a carefully packaged "human" equality.

Nevertheless, prison detention, removing Thuku and Kenyatta from the mainstream of the people's struggles, was the essential first step in their total repudiation of former militancy, making them say yes to that which only yesterday was most repugnant to their seemingly progressive selves.

3

The other type of political prisoner, typified by Waiyaki wa Hinga, Ngunju wa Gakere, Me Katilili, and Arap Manyei,[5] never repudiated their former militant political stands. Led down the ladder of despair by the demons of surrender, they turned their eyes away from the valley of white bones and looked up to their people's history and culture of struggle and determination and gained the strength to say no to the colonial culture of fear and its ethic of submissive silence. They were sure that a million hands united in struggle would finally break the rock of oppression. They as individuals could go, but the struggle would continue, and they would forever be part of it. Detention and imprisonment couldn't break their spirits; it could at most break their bodies. So they remained firm, defiant, and strong. In the zenith of colonial culture, this kind of political prisoner was labeled a hard-core Mau Mau.

Now to the original list of Waiyaki, Me Katilili, Arap Manyei, and Kenya Land and Freedom Army hard-core anti-imperialists, we may add two more political prisoners, Makhan Singh and J.M. Kariũki. The list grows with time.

The positive contribution of Kenyan workers of Asian origin to the struggle for independence has been deliberately played down by European colonialists and their Kenyan intellectual sympathizers and chauvinists of all shades. From 1893 to the present, Indian workers, Indian labor leaders, and progressive Indian newspaper editors have contributed a lot to Kenya's anti-imperialist struggle.[6]

The name of Makhan Singh, a remarkable Kenyan of Asian origins, is synonymous with the growth of a modern workers' movement and progressive trade unionism. We see him in successive stages as the able and dedicated general secretary of the Indian Trade Union, the Labour Trade Union of Kenya, and the East African Trade Union Congress. Like Thuku in the 1920s, he correctly saw the economic emancipation of workers in political terms. Strikes were legitimate weapons of political struggle.

Indeed, the right to strike was a worker's basic human right: it was only the enslaved, because it has been taken away from them, who had no right to bargain for what they should be given for the use of their labor power. If a worker is unable to strike, then he is in the position of the enslaved.

One of the resolutions proposed by Makhan Singh and adopted by the Trade Union Congress at Kaloleni Hall in Nairobi on April 23, 1950, was a demand for the complete independence and sovereignty of the East African territories, as the only way in which workers could get a fair economic deal. On May 1, 1950, Makhan Singh wrote:

The call of May Day 1950, in the middle of the twentieth century, is that the workers and the peoples of East Africa should further strengthen their unity, should become more resolute and thus speed up the movement for freedom of all the workers and peoples of East Africa.

He was arrested on May 15, 1950, and was prosecuted by Anthony George Somerhough in the court of Ransley Samuel Thacker, the same colonialist duo who were later to sit in judgment over Jomo Kenyatta and the rest of the Kapenguria Six.

In the colonial court, Makhan Singh carried himself with calm dignity, answering all the racist provocation of the prosecution with a progressive political line that further maddened Thacker and Somerhough. When, for instance, Singh told the kangaroo court that the British government had no right to rule Kenya, that the country should have a workers' government with a parliament freely elected by the people and answerable only to the country's workers and peasants through their organizations, the settler magistrate was so outraged that he took over the role of prosecution:

THACKER: Where would you get your judges, for instance?

SINGH: From the people of this country.

THACKER: There is no single African qualified in law?

SINGH: The new government will give opportunities for training people to become judges, lawyers, magistrates, etc.

THACKER: In the present stage of the African, you would be content to appoint him a judge or magistrate?

SINGH: Of course. If before the advent of the British they were able to judge about matters, even now they can do it.

Makhan Singh was imprisoned in Lokitaung, Maralal, and Dol Dol for eleven and a half years, from June 5, 1950, to October 22, 1961. During that time, he was constantly visited by the demons in the physical form of prison officers, district commissioners, and other colonial agents, who tried to pressure him into agreeing to leave Kenya and be rewarded for it, or to recant and start working against the Kenya workers' movement and progressive nationalism, with rewards of course, but he refused.

After his release, he resumed his activities in the workers' movement. His book, *Kenya's Trade Union Movement to 1951*, is, up to now, the only progressive treatment of the emergence of modern Kenya.

It is clear that even Makhan Singh, of Asian origin, derived his strength to say no from his roots in the progressive aspects of Kenyan people's culture. In an article he wrote for the *Daily Chronicle* of February 12, 1949, he urged Kenyans of Asian origin to forge common links with native Kenyans. "The main task before us," he wrote, "is to forge a strong unity among ourselves and with Africans for the common cause of democratic advance in this country." He advocated the establishment of common schools for all Kenyans. "Learn the language of the people—Swahili. Teach the best of your culture, learn the best from African culture. This way lies our salvation and this is the way out!"

J.M. Kariūki has written an account of his own wrestling bouts with demons in at least fourteen concentration camps all over Kenya. His autobiography, *Mau Mau Detainee*, is an important contribution to the Kenyan literature of struggle, and I have written about it in my book *Writers in Politics* (Heinemann Educational Books, London). In Manyani, the European camp commandant sadistically tortured Kariūki to make him sign a statement of submissive acquiescence and betrayal. But Kariŭki said *no*. "I was given the strength to endure all these things," he later wrote, "because I knew that I was right. . . . This is the sort of strength that no amount of beatings can weaken."

Even the glamorous easy riches of independence—for the lucky few—couldn't deflect him from the path of struggle. He became one of the bitterest critics of the postindependence betrayal of Kenyan people. He kept reminding Kenyatta and the entire KANU leadership that it takes more than a flag and an anthem to make a nation. "We don't want to create a Kenya of ten millionaires and ten million beggars," he would add, in stark contrast to Kenyatta's refrain, "What have you done for yourself?"

Like Makhan Singh before him, Kariŭki had dared to say no.

4

Makhan Singh was a communist. He said so both before and after his detention and imprisonment. As such, he was opposed to capitalism. J.M. Kariŭki was a nationalist. He was not necessarily opposed to capitalism. He wanted to free national capitalism from foreign control and to build a welfare state in which "everyone will have an opportunity to educate himself to his fullest capabilities, in which no one will die or suffer through lack of medical facilities and in which each person will earn enough to eat for himself and his family."

However, they shared a common anti-imperialist national tradition that goes way back to the very early political prisoners—Me Katilili, Waiyaki, Ngunju wa Gakere—who all said no to the colonial culture of fear and rejected its aesthetic of blind trust and obedience to foreign economic, political, and cultural occupation and encirclement. On the contrary, they had rooted themselves in the people's revolutionary culture of outspoken courage and patriotic heroism, a tradition that Kariũki invoked when as a youth he took the oath of loyalty to Kenya Land and Freedom Army. Afterward, in the maize, he wrote in *Mau Mau Detainee*:

> I felt exalted with a new spirit of power and strength. All my previous life seemed empty and meaningless. Even my education, of which I was so proud, appeared trivial besides this splendid and terrible force that had been given me. I had been born again and I sensed once more the feeling of opportunity and adventure that I had on the first day my mother started teaching me to read and write. The other three in the maize were all silent and were clearly undergoing the same spiritual rebirth as myself.

Armed with the new power given him by his total identification with the resistance culture of his people, he was able to face imprisonment and all the temptations in the stony wilderness. Detention could not break him. Only death. But that came later, not at the hands of a colonial commandant in a concentration camp but at the hands of those who had inherited the colonial power.

In 1953 he was taken from his own small hotel in Nakuru to the first of more than fourteen concentration camps, where he endured seven years of torture. In 1975 he was arrested inside a prominent foreign-owned hotel in Nairobi. After hours of torture, he was sent to a death camp at Ngong.

A colonial affair . . . a neocolonial affair—what's the difference?

5

It was not very cheering to know that most of those who had said no to the culture of fear died untimely deaths, buried alive in deserts or left on hillsides for hyenas' midnight feasts. Nor was it pleasant to contemplate that I was now in detention under a regime headed by an ex–political prisoner who had finally given in to years of imperialist pressure. Would a political yes-man ever recognize the rights of a political no-man and the human and democratic legitimacy and necessity of that position? Would he, in other words, release a political prisoner who dared say no where he himself had said yes?

Yes. No. *Ndio. La.* Two of the tiniest words in any language. But one had to choose between them. To say yes or no to unfairness, injustice, wrongdoing, oppression, treacherous betrayal, the culture of fear, and the aesthetic of submissive acquiescence, one was choosing a particular world and a future.

Wasonga Sijeyo's position inspired both hope and despair. He had refused to renounce his pre-1969 anti-imperialist and anti-exploitation views and he was now entering his tenth year at Kamĩtĩ. Others were in their eighth, seventh, fourth, or third year. I was only just starting. That Wuodh Sijeyo looked cheerful and strong in spirit was a source of hope, but that he was now in his tenth year with no hints of release was cause for despair. If release for those who said no depended on the number of years, what hope was there for us who were novices? There came a time when virtually all of us eighteen political prisoners silently said, *Let them release Wasonga Sijeyo, at least; that would signal hope for us too!*

I am not trying to write a story of heroism. I am only a scribbler of words. Pen and paper have so far been my only offensive and defensive weapons against those who would like to drown human speech in a pool of fear—or blood. Besides, I would hate to court unnecessary martyrdom. But I searched every corner of my mind and heart to see if I could find a speck of wrongdoing in joining hands with Kamīrīthū peasants and workers in our open democratic venture of building our village, and I could find not the slightest trace of wrong to challenge my conscience.

If release depended on duration of stay, I was in for a long spell. If it depended on saying yes, then I was likewise in for a long stay in Kamītī or any other prison in Kenya. For right from the beginning, I was determined never to renounce Kamīrīthū—there was really too much of Limuru and Kenyan history in that tiny village! I was equally resolved to always speak truthfully and proudly about our collective aims and achievements at Kamīrīthū Community Education and Cultural Centre. I would never, for as long as I lived, and for as long as I was sane, disown the heroic history of Kenyan people as celebrated in *Ngaahika Ndeenda*, or be a conscious party to the historical betrayal mourned and condemned in the same drama. My involvement with the people of Kamīrīthū had given me the sense of having become a new being, and it had made me transcend the alienation to which I had been condemned by years of colonial education.

So I was intellectually reconciled to the possibility of a long stay in prison. If Wasonga Sijeyo was the yardstick, then the earliest release date I could think of was 1988. No thought for comfort. Besides, intellectual acceptance was one thing; emotional reconciliation to the stark reality was another. I had to find ways and means of keeping my sanity. Writing a novel was one way.

I came up with a tentative ten-year writing plan. I would finish the Gĩkũyũ version of the one I was writing by the end of 1978. Gĩkũyũ was the language of my birth. Then I would embark on a Swahili version in 1979. Kiswahili was the all-Kenya national language, with its roots in the culture of Kenya's coastal nationalities. In 1980, I would attempt an English version. English was a foreign language, but it was an important language in the history of Kenya. All this was in line with my new language policy.

Thereafter? Maybe I would find other things with which to occupy myself. Besides, one could never really tell how long a novel would take to write. *The River Between* had taken me one year; *Weep not, Child*, two; *A Grain of Wheat*, three; and *Petals of Blood*, about four years. Maybe the new novel, translations included, would take me many years. Or it might never be completed. For I would continue to write in Gĩkũyũ, and under prison conditions, where one had to keep on playing a game of write-and-hide, with inquisitive guards prying and prowling constantly.

But writing aside, I knew, in my heart of hearts that my sanity depended on my being able to continually say no to any and every manifestation of injustice and to any and every infringement of my human and democratic rights, a no that included detention itself. I would seize any and every occasion to denounce detention and imprisonment without trial. Yes or no—two great words in their own way, but the greater of them was no when spoken in sound or silence or action against oppression.

In Kamĩtĩ prison, one of the most oppressive and offensive practices to human dignity was the chaining of political prisoners before giving them medical treatment or letting them see their wives and children. Those who had the misfortune of being hospitalized received even worse treatment. In the operating room, their legs and hands were chained to bed frames while armed police officers and prison guards stood on guard night and day.

The other political prisoners had told me about this, and I dreaded the prospect of this unnecessary humiliation. It was not so much the chaining that I minded most—one had no power to resist if it was forced on one; it was the expectation and requirement of a political prisoner's own cooperation in the rituals of his own enslavement that I found most repugnant. Cooperate in my own chaining as the condition for getting medical treatment that I was entitled to, and as the condition for a five-minute glance at my wife in the presence of an overarmed escort?

Then a tooth begun to hurt, intermittently at first and then rising to a continuous throb. The prison doctor recommended that I see a dentist at Kenyatta National Hospital. I could not delay the confrontation I dreaded.

6

Unchain My Hands!

1

Jela ilimshinda, or *alishindwa na jela*, meaning "prison defeated him," was an expression often on the lips of guards, discrediting any political prisoner who had physically or mentally broken down within the double-walled compound, almost as if they—the guards—were some neutral referees in a gladiatorial contest between the prison and the prisoner, a contest that the defcated had freely and willingly entered with the sure-to-win braggadocio of a Muhammad Ali.

The expression was a cover for any fatal or near-fatal ill treatment of a political prisoner: the moral accountability for the disablement is thus thrust back onto the victim, like Karen Blixen's magistrate holding the murdered Kitosch responsible for his own death because he had moaned in pain, "Nataka kufa" (I would rather die).

But the guards' pretense of a contest between prison and prisoner, with cheering or jeering forces behind each, also contains a grain of truth. A narration of prison life is nothing more than an account of oppressive measures in varying degrees of intensity and the individual or collective responses to them. Even if one were getting the best possible food, accommodations, and health care, the fact of being wrongfully held in captivity at presidential pleasure, the forcible seizure of a person for an indefinite time entirely determined by somebody else's fears, is in itself torture, and it is continuous torture to the last second of one's detention. All other forms of torture, not excepting the physical, pale beside this cruelest of the state-inflicted wounds upon one's humanity.

The imprisoning authorities are not, of course, content to just inflict the wound once; they must keep twisting hot knives into it to ensure its continued freshness. This re-infliction takes various forms: beatings with the constant possibility of being beaten to death, straitjacketing for total bodily immobility, being made to sleep on cold or wet cement floors without a mat or a blanket so the body can more easily contract disease, denial of news or books to weaken the intellect, bestial food or a starvation diet to weaken the body, segregation and solitary confinement to weaken the heart—these and more are the standard sadisms of prisons and concentration camps. One or a combination of these instruments can be used to keep the wound fresh. And for the duration of the presidential pleasure, the stony dragon remains deaf to all human cries and groans from its captives.

Saint Man in a deadly combat with the stony dragon: not for comfort the thought that nobody can tell beforehand how he or she will cope with the unsought-for combat. Nobody knows how long the president's pleasure might last. Nobody can tell how a particular prisoner will physically, intellectually, and spiritually survive the hot knives of torture.

Many factors come into it: stamina, the occasional measure of fairness and humaneness in the guards and prison officers, the extent and intensity of the jailers' desire to break their victim, and the degree of the detainee's awareness of and commitment to the cause that brought that person to jail. More important are the prisoner's moral standards and principles born of that awareness and commitment. Anitar, an African poet of Arabia, once wrote that despite captivity in slavery:

> I will not leave a word for the railers
> And I will not ease the hearts of my enemies
> by the violation of my honour.
> I have borne with misfortune till I have
> discovered its secret meaning.

Even with such ideals, however, it is hard to predict one's bodily or mental reactions to certain forms of torture. Some people can withstand any amount of physical torture; others, any amount of psychological torture; and a few others can withstand all without breaking, even unto death. Kindness can break some; threats, others. Whatever the case, one can tell this only at the hour of trial.

At Kamĩtĩ, disease and family were the two most frequent means of tormenting political prisoners. First, disease. It was the most dreaded hydra in Kamĩtĩ Prison. "Whatever you do," the other political prisoners had told me, "try not to be ill. . . . Here they wait until disease has fully percolated through your system before treating you, . . . and even then, they treat you not to cure, but to have it on record that they treated you."

One political prisoner suffered swollen veins. His laments

would be met with indifference or with the catch-all charge of malingering. Then suddenly he would be whisked off to Kenyatta National Hospital, in chains, under heavy guard, for surgery. Two days later, he would be back in the block, still in chains, but with bleeding cuts. The laments would start all over again. This game of treatment-without-curing had gone on for seven years. He was still hospitalized at Kenyatta National Hospital when news of his freedom reached him.

Another political prisoner had a wound in the anus: advanced piles. He bled a lot. He had to lie sideways. Eating was torture because of thoughts of the pain to follow. He had been arrested a week before he was due for an operation by a top specialist at Kenyatta National Hospital. His terror was that the wound might extend to his intestines. On arrival at Kamĩtĩ, he had reported his critical condition. It was not until six months later that they took him to hospital for an operation. He could hardly walk. But they put him in chains, plus an armed police and prison squad. At the time of his release on December 12, 1978, he was still uncured.

My own observation was that at Kamĩtĩ, every political prisoner suffered from one or more diseases: headaches, backaches, toothaches, eye and skin ailments, anything. And the guards had only one explanation, malingering, although there was no work to be avoided. The prison doctor, a man who had been in prison all his working life, had only one explanation: depression. The standard prescription for everything, headaches, stomachaches, toothaches, broken backs and hips, was antidepression tablets—Valium, mostly. "It's just the effect of jail," he would say. "You'll soon come out." He normally met complaints with a chilling threat: "I can even inject you with water or worse and get away with it. You think you're more important than Kenyatta whom I used to treat with water at Lodwar?" He was an example of the continuity of the colonial into the postcolonial.

The most notorious case of disease as punishment was Shikuku's. Martin Shikuku was a populist, a vocal member of parliament who had made a national reputation for himself by raising awkward issues in the "House of the Honourables." He was an active member of the committee formed to investigate the case of J.M. Kariũki, the findings and final report of which virtually incriminated the Kenyatta regime in Kariũki's torture and assassination. He also proposed and won a motion for a select committee on corruption, causing much hatred from the big ones, who proceeded to quash it. Then one day in October 1975, he made a passing reference to the effect that parliament should not be killed the way KANU had been killed. He was detained and put in prison.

I had mentioned his detention and that of Jean-Marie Seroney in my novel *Petals of Blood*, so I was naturally curious to see him. One day, soon after my arrival in Kamĩtĩ, I entered his cell. I found him seated on the bed. There was a yellow plastic pail near him. Between every two sentences, he would vomit into the pail. Each time he belched, he would vomit into it. He had to eat about fifteen times a day so that after vomiting something would remain behind to sustain his life. He had been in that condition for two years. I was shaken by this revelation. He was a very sick man really, although he took it all philosophically. "That which is hidden under the bed will one day come to light," he told me. I could never have believed the scene in a supposedly independent Kenya. Why keep a sick man in prison just to prove to him that the ruling party was not dead, that what he thought was death was simply the party's style of life? I was then under internal segregation and the guard ordered me back to my cell.

I was looking through the iron bars of my door when suddenly I saw somebody crawling along the corridor, using the walls for support. What apparition was this? It was Shikuku again. He had come to ask me a few questions about the outside. Now I learned that on top of his minute-after-minute vomiting, the man could not walk without support. There was something wrong with his hips. To the guards? He was malingering. To the doctor? He was simply depressed. Although he could not walk without some support, Shikuku used to be chained to his bed in the hospital, with armed police and warders guarding all the exits and entrances night and day. He remained in that tortured condition, the doctors unable to cure him, the authorities unwilling to let him go home and seek his own cure. The instructions to the stony dragon concerning the detained combatant would seem to have been: if you miss his *will*, don't miss his *body*. Break his *will*, or break his *body* or both.

Not surprisingly, fear of illness was itself another kind of disease infecting all the political prisoners at Kamĩtĩ. Along with it was also the fear of being poisoned under the pretext of being treated. I too caught the fever. What I dreaded most was a possible recurrence of my asthma. In Dakar, Senegal, in 1968, I had nearly lost my life after a very severe attack, my inability to speak French hindering my frantic efforts to get a doctor or any medical help. The timely arrival of Ali Mazrui in my hotel had saved me. At home in Limuru, I always kept some quick-relief tablets in readiness. At Kamĩtĩ prison, I was lucky. Not once did I get such an attack, not even bronchial wheezes, but the fear remained.

It was the toothache that caught me unawares. The rearmost lower right-side molar had a hole, and I started experiencing difficulties in eating. The right side was really very painful, and woe unto the whole mouth if a grain of salt should lodge itself in the hollow. However, when the doctor recommended that I see a dentist at Kenyatta National Hospital, I was seized with panic.

Two principles suddenly clashed inside me: the necessity for bodily fitness for my physical survival in the combat and the necessity to make a stand over the issue of chains for my spiritual survival in the combat.

2

It is the paramount duty of all political prisoners to keep physically fit. Any bodily disablement can considerably weaken their will or forever damage them. Those who survive the deadly combat can always live to fight another day. There is also the saying, told me by one political prisoner as a piece of homely advice: When a cow is finally pinned to the ground and tied with ropes, it cannot refuse to be slaughtered. We in detention were that cow, and we had no choice but to do whatever was dictated by the whims of our captors.

But a human being is not a dumb beast. Even the cow does not acquiesce in its own slaughter. It goes down kicking to the last breath. In the same way, political prisoners must always stand for certain principles to prop their spirits in the struggle to survive the trials of the stony dragon. They must be ready to protest against wrongs even in prison. They must keep on insisting on their constitutional rights, however few and whatever they are, and on their democratic and human rights.

Now my own feelings were that, once the authorities had detained a person, they carried the entire responsibility for any diseases afflicting that person for the simple reason that prisoners cannot take care of themselves medically. I felt that it was wrong, it was criminal in fact, to torture people with disease, to use it to extort information or confession, to use it as a means of vindictive humiliation or to break a person's will. I strongly felt that if the authorities were unable to take a prisoner to a hospital outside the compound, then, even by the least of all democratic and human fairness, they had to bring a doctor into the compound. Even prisoners of war are supposed to be given full and fair medical treatment without conditions.

In Kenya, particularly at Kamĩtĩ, it was a different story. Crawl on your hands and feet so that we can treat you. Cooperate in your own chains of humiliation without a murmur of protest so that we can take you to the hospital. Kneel and beg; if not, die or become crippled forever. Quite apart from that, I had resolved that, at the earliest possible moment, I would make my feelings known about the whole business of chaining political prisoners, people who had never been convicted in a court of law, who never had any history of physical violence, escape, or attempted escape.

The same political prisoner who had advised me on the necessity for passivity at a slaughterhouse told me that chains on the innocent were badges of honor, and a political prisoner should never be afraid of them. No. Chains were badges of humiliation. But I was not afraid of them. After all, I had come to Kamītī in them. Even if I had been chained and dragged through the streets of Nairobi or my village, I would never have allowed the intended humiliation to touch my heart, because I had done no wrong whatsoever. I had merely chosen sides in the class struggle. To write for, speak for, and work for the lives of peasants and workers was the highest call of national duty. My only regret was that for many years I had wandered in the bourgeois jungle and the wilderness of foreign cultures and languages. Kamīrīthū was my homecoming.

Nevertheless, I had resolved that, while I wouldn't make any physical resistance to the wearing of chains—that way lay suicide—I would equally not willingly or cooperatively put out my hands for chaining. I would at least say no. I would kick even though I was tied up and being led to a slaughterhouse.

I knew this course might involve me in certain difficulties. The tendency is for a police or prison officer to take such a protest as a personal affront or defiance of his own personality. I had to keep reminding myself that when the time came, I should protest politely but firmly. I should state my case without rudeness to the executing authority, for my being at Kamītī was not a directly personal thing between him and me.

For a long time before the dreaded day, I keenly felt this clash of principles. I wished that the battlefield had not been my health. But I equally felt that if I didn't say no to this oppressive requirement at the earliest opportunity, I would never thereafter be able to say no over the same issue or any other acts of blatant oppression.

Then the hour suddenly came. Thursday, June 15, 1978. Over

three months after my initial complaint of toothaches. At Kamĩtĩ a political prisoner was told he was going out only a few minutes before the police armed escort was due to arrive. The political prisoner was then required to change from his prison uniform, *kũngũrũ*, into his civilian clothes, which were otherwise kept under lock and key in the chief warder's office.

It was about ten in the morning. I changed as required. I walked through the compound toward the gates. Was it worth resisting the chains? I have said no to oppression several times in my life, and I have always experienced the same sensation of agonizing fears and doubts, before voicing or acting my protest. I feel foolish, childish even . . . why disturb the currents?

As a boy, I used to pick pyrethrum flowers for one of the very few African landlords in pre-independence Limuru. The landlord on whose land we lived as *muhoi* tenant-at-will had an orchard of pears and plums. Once, some children went into the orchard and picked a few plums. The landlord's wife came to know about it. In the evening, after she had weighed our flowers with a spring balance, she announced that we would all lose our day's pay in punishment for the stolen plums. It was a collective punishment, but of course if we squealed and pointed out the culprits, or if the offenders gave themselves up voluntarily, then the innocents would be spared. We were all angry because of the collective punishment and its severity: lose a whole day's pay because of a few "stolen" plums? She called out each person's name. Own up to the crime, squeal, or lose your day's work! She was met with noncommittal silence.

My heart was beating hard. Gĩkũyũ precolonial culture, the remnants of which still governed our lives, was very strict about the relationship between a child and a grown-up. I remember, for instance, being admonished by my mother for telling an adult, to his face, that he was lying. Grown-ups had the right to beat a child who was rude to them, even if they were the ones who had initiated the action resulting in the rude exchange. And if the grown-up should report such an exchange to the parents, woe unto the "rude" child. I now believe that the oppressive reactionary tendencies in our pre-colonial peasant cultures are only slightly less grave than the racist colonial culture of fear and silence and that they should be fought, maybe with different weapons, but fought all the same. But I had not then worked this out.

I felt cold panic inside me. I knew I would raise a dissenting voice. I was stung by the injustice of it all, and although I could not reverse it, I had no intention of suffering in silence. In our home, we depended on every single cent that we could collect from the sale of our labor. We had sweated in the sun, without a meal or a glass of water all day, and here she was, going on about morality and enforcing it by robbing us of our hard-earned money without so much as a blink. "You claim you are saved," I shouted at her in tears. "Is this what you mean by Christian salvation? Cheating and robbing us? This is theft! This is theft!" She came to my home the same night and reported what she called this "terrible abuse from a mere child" and urged my mother to beat me. My mother, a peasant living on the estate of the landlord, just looked down. She didn't say anything. But she didn't beat me.

I had felt the same cold panic each time I knew I would join the chorus of those at the university who used to protest against the annual beating of protesting students, a yearly ritual of violence fully sanctioned by government. The worst such ritual was in 1974, when women were raped and others had their limbs broken, their blood left spattered all over the whitewashed walls of the different classrooms. In 1969, I had resigned from the university in protest. I was outraged by the silence of most lecturers and professors, a silence that I took for complicity with the fascist evil. But in 1974 more lecturers had joined in the protest and had made their feelings publicly known.

What I most remembered about these past incidents was that unpleasant cold foreboding that always preceded my every *no* to oppression, but it was always a sign that I would not hold back the voice of protest. So when now the prison guard asked me to raise my hands for the ceremony of chaining and I felt the same kind of foreboding, I knew I would refuse. Which I did!

The guard, also in civilian clothes—going out for a political prisoner was a civilian ceremony all around—couldn't believe his ears. He called the others. Still I refused.

He reasoned with me, trying to prove to me that the chains meant nothing: "Be a man and carry the chains!"

I thought this a strange way of proving my "manhood," and if there was nothing to the chains, why was I required to wear them? I still refused.

Kimeto, the police superintendent in charge of escorting political prisoners in and out of Kamĩtĩ, intervened. He was tall, with a partiality for straw hats, which he wore with a conscious swagger, probably in imitation of an American FBI detective he had once seen on television.

"Listen!" he said, standing arms akimbo, measuring his

voice for all to hear clearly. "Even Kenyatta was once chained, and he accepted it."

"I am not Kenyatta!" I said.

"So you refuse to go for medical treatment?"

"Would I have so promptly put on my civilian clothes if I was not eager to go? After all, it is I who have the toothache. It is you who is refusing to take me to hospital."

"Then we have to chain you."

"I don't want to be chained. I don't see why you must chain an innocent political prisoner."

"You are refusing to go to hospital."

"No. It is you, refusing to take me. I am not faster than all the bullets you and your team are carrying. Why anyway chain me as a condition for medical treatment? If you are finding it difficult to take me out to see a dentist, and I am not insisting on going out, why don't you bring a dentist here?"

"Take him back to the cell!" he shouted, disgust written all over his detective face. "We shall see if he will cure himself."

I was never treated, though I kept on complaining. I even complained to the commissioner of prisons, Mutua, on the only occasion that he visited the compound. I pointed out that it was wrong to use disease to torture political prisoners.

I also wrote a letter of protest to Mūhīndī Mūnene, the political prisoners' security officer, seeking his intervention to secure me dental treatment inside the compound. It had been done before, I later came to learn, so there was nothing in the regulations that said that a dentist couldn't come into Kamītī. Nor was there a regulation requiring chaining as a condition for medical treatment outside Kamītī. Even if there was, it was unjust and criminal. Not all political prisoners, I came to learn, were chained!

Mr. Mũnene never replied. And the Detainees Review Tribunal under the Honourable Mister Justice Alan Robin Winston Hancox, before whom I raised the matter in July, never did anything about the use of disease to torture political prisoners.

One got the impression that the next stage for the authorities would be to actually infect political prisoners with certain diseases if natural ones failed. Any political prisoner who contracted a disease and was taken to the hospital or was treated in prison had always that additional fear. What if, having got there, the government quack "mistakenly" injected strychnine, causing death not in combat or in defiance but prostrate in a ward bed? Considering Kenya's recent history and the general official attitude toward disease, this fear was not without foundation.

Fortunately for me, the abscess gradually healed—must have been the medicine of willpower. At any rate, it gradually ceased throbbing except when something hard—like a grain of salt or a piece of bean or *ugali*—lodged inside it.

But this was not the end of the chains affair. The next act was later to be played out on the occasion of a scheduled family visit six months after my abduction.

3

Because of the intensity of emotion attached to it, the family can be used to break the political backbone of an unprepared political prisoner. Any forcible separation from loved ones is, of course, very painful, but even more painful is the sense of utter helplessness. There is nothing one can do about it. Such a person feels that there was something left unsaid, a sentence cut off in the middle, a melody abruptly stopped. It now feels as if even a minute's brief reunion would enable the unsaid to be said, the sentence or the melody completed. If only . . . if . . . if . . .

In my case, I had left Nyambura four months pregnant, and now a child, whom I could see only through the courtesy of photography and the post office, had been born. A visit would enable me to see her. I was also eager to know how the others—Thiong'o, Kīmunya, Ngīna, Ndūcū, Mūkoma, and Wanjikū—were doing at school and how they were taking the whole thing. My mother also. In 1955 she had to bear three months of torture at a Kamīrīthū Home Guard post because of my elder brother, who had joined the Kenya Land and Freedom Army guerrillas. Throughout the 1950s, she had to carry the burden of not knowing if he would come out of the mountains, and later out of the concentration camps, alive. In 1974 she lost her youngest son, Njinjū, in a car accident. I knew that now she would be very afraid of losing another. A visit would reassure her. As for Nyambura, I was keen to erase from my mind my last image of her: standing in the inner corridor of our house at Gītogothi, pregnant, bewildered, but silent in absolute immobility. "Give me the keys of the car!" were her last words before they took me away. She had seen what I was not able to see: that they were taking me away for a long time.

Spouses may not understand why their loved ones—wives, husbands, sons, and daughters—were arrested or may not sympathize with the cause. Such a person can easily be approached directly or indirectly—through a third or fourth party, that is—and be fed, in a sympathetic tone and voice, stories of the loved one's arrogance or stubbornness in prison, of how the loved one has spurned all the government's moves for reconciliation and cooperation. The left-behinds will be told, ever so earnestly, that their husband/son/wife/daughter is behaving as if they *are* the government or own the government. It might then be suggested to them that a letter from them, just a few lines urging the prisoner to cooperate, could work miracles and hasten their release. Examples of those already released can be referred to: "Is your husband/son/wife/daughter bigger than so-and-so, who agreed to cooperate and was immediately released? Look at him now. He's the director of this or that government crop-marketing board or this or that parastatal corporation. Why can't your husband/son/wife/daughter agree to come out of prison and play the same kind of constructive role?"

Before they are aware of what's happening, the tables are turned and subject/object relationships are reversed. It is the husband/wife/son/daughter who is now stubbornly clinging to the prison walls despite several magnanimous government pleas. Gradually the person on the outside will be put in the position of thinking that their spouse is actively working for and aiding their own release by writing them letters gently, lovingly rebuking them for their uncooperativeness. They might even add stories of family suffering and how the prisoner's presence is urgently needed if the home is not going to fall apart. An exchange of letters (the prisoner's censored, of course) might start here, but these will only widen the gulf of mutual incomprehension.

On the side of the detained person, stories of the spouse's

moral conduct in their absence might be leaked to the prisoner. If they are people of property, the victim may be allowed to know how everything they had spent so much toil and sweat and years to build is going to ruins.

There was a guard who, whenever it was his turn at night, would come to my door and would literally insist that it was I who was refusing to leave prison. "You know the government cannot bring you here for nothing. Just own up, confess everything . . . and you'll see yourself home tomorrow, but go on demanding to know why you were detained and, my friend, you will be here forever." The guard knew the Limuru area very well, and I often wondered what stories such a person might be releasing about my stubborn refusal to be "free."

Therefore, when political prisoners get a chance to see their spouses and families, they are very eager to seize the time, because even though they will have no privacy, they can reassure the family and give them the heart and spirit to endure the trials to come. Prisoners also gain strength and spirit from that brief supervised encounter. All the words that could be said cannot not be said, the sentence and the melody remain incomplete, but another word will have been added, another note will have been sung.

What I found disgusting in these family visits were the elaborate lies in the whole surreal exercise. First the family, not the prisoner, had to apply for a visit through the political prisoners' security officer or through the Ministry of Home Affairs. Depending on the whims of the concerned authorities—there really seemed to be no rational basis for granting or denying these visits—the family would be notified to call at the necessary police station early in the morning of a particular day.

They would then be driven to the airport and ushered into a waiting room. They would wait for hours.

Meanwhile, at Kamĩtĩ, the "lucky" political prisoner would be given half an hour's notice to get ready to see his dear ones. He would quickly change into his civilian clothes (released from custody for the purpose), rush to the gates for the usual chaining ceremony by a contingent of armed police officers, and be driven in a blinds-drawn police vehicle to the door of the waiting room.

There, the chains would be removed, and he would be ushered into the waiting room for a five-minute chat with his spouse, surrounded on all sides by security men and civilian-clad prison guards. Then he would be whisked out of the room, put back into chains, and be driven back to Kamĩtĩ under heavy escort, to resume life in prison uniform. Thus without knowing it, the prisoner had participated in a gigantic lie to his family and to the entire Kenyan nation. Family members would now spread the lie that their relative had come by plane from a distant place. He was in civilian clothes, so therefore he was not really in prison and probably was not being treated badly after all.

I used to look at the faces of the political prisoners just before and after the visits. On going, they were all smiles. On coming back, they were all depression. They would carry their private grief on their faces for a few weeks more before hiding it inside and resuming the communal, contourless monotony of prison life. A family visit was not really a contact; it was more a renewal of the sorrow of separation.

But my main concern, even for the cherished family visits at the airport rendezvous, was still with the chains one was required to wear. I resolved that either they would let me see my family without chaining me as a condition, or they would not allow me to see them. At any rate, I was determined that, while I would participate in the charade of putting on civilian clothes, I certainly would not willingly accept the chains. I still had not yet developed wings faster than the bullets they all carried in their guns.

When the day and the hour finally came—again unexpected, just half an hour or so for changing clothes—I found that all the prison officers in charge of the compound were present. Plus a police contingent led by the escorting police superintendent with his American swagger, straw hat, and arms akimbo stance. Most of the other political prisoners had crowded into the compound. Now one of the prison officers came to my cell and shut the door behind him. He started lecturing me, as to a little child, about the virtues of family visits and how much good they did to all those concerned.

"Imagine all the little ones coming all that way and finding out that their daddy has refused to see them. I know you may want to prove to all these other political prisoners that you can stick to your principles. Principles are all right. But it is your wife and children you are going to see, and you shouldn't care a damn how these others are going to view it. Some of these political prisoners, and I am telling you this in confidence, have only themselves to blame for their nonrelease . . . so obstinate. . . . Now these chains, they are really nothing, nothing at all. . . . Just be a man. . . . I wouldn't want you to lose all the sympathy some people have for you."

I listened to his monologue with all its suggestive hints, vague promises, and veiled threats, all harmonized into an avuncular plea for me to show common sense and willingly accept the chains. I politely thanked him for his advice and concern, but I reiterated my position that I would not accept wearing chains as a condition of seeing my family. It was almost a repetition of the earlier scene. I walked to the gates. I refused to wear the chains. They refused to let me see my family.

For weeks after, I was literally trembling inside, wondering what lies had been fed Nyambura and the children. I was not particularly worried about how my peasant mother would take it. I knew that from her experiences during the British-imposed State of Emergency, she would never believe the police version of events.

But Nyambura? And the children? It was a terrible three weeks; some of the political prisoners reproached me in silence, as if I had taken a joke too far, while a few others told me so to my face. How dare you refuse to see your family? How do you think they will take your stubborn refusal? Why increase their misery?

With these, I would patiently go over the arguments. I would tell them that I had not refused but that I had not been allowed. I would reiterate my strong feelings about the chaining of political prisoners. I would explain the necessity of struggling for democratic and human rights even in prison. I would explain the importance of a truly democratic Kenya in which the different classes and nationalities would freely debate the past, present, and future of our country without fear or favor or flattery. This democratic Kenya would not be given to people on a silver platter by the ruling minority class. It had to be struggled for. Kenyan people, wherever they were, under whatever circumstances, had to keep on insisting on certain irreducible democratic and human rights. If we did not do this, if we all succumbed to the culture of fear and silence, Kenya would have merely moved from a colonial prison into a neocolonial prison, while the more than seventy years' struggle was precisely to release Kenyan people from economic, political, and cultural prison altogether. What was the real gain in moving from one prison, run by white guards, into the same prison now run by black guards? The difference was one of form and not of substance. The point really was to change the economic, political, and cultural substance, and this would never be possible without a struggle for democracy. This struggle was not a mere verbal abstraction. It had to begin where each Kenyan was: in our homes, in our schools, in our places of work, even in prisons.

There were a few, though, who understood my position, and they told me so. They even told me that chaining political prisoners was a recent development. It had not always been the practice. When Edward P. Lokopoyet first introduced it, they had tried to organize a collective stand against it, but a few political prisoners developed cold feet at the very last minute and readily jumped into the chains. They pointed out that, as a result of the disunity, now they were all exposed to extreme danger, especially when they traveled by air to Mombasa, because even in the plane they were still in chains!

But my main worry was still Nyambura and the children. I knew that I could never write down my version of events, because this would certainly be censored by the police and the prison authorities.

Then one day I received a letter from her. It was the best

gift I could have gotten from anybody, but coming from her, from home, from my family, it touched my heart. I shut myself in my cell and studied every word, line, and paragraph to get at the unstated message. The letter, written after the airport fiasco, was in reply to another I had written months before on receiving news of Njoki's birth. Now she referred to that letter and deliberately avoided references to the visit. Not a word of rebuke. No complaint. That in itself was a vote of confidence. . . . I read it over and over again:

> Greetings from *your big family*. We are safe and sound. The children are still growing. Particularly our new baby. She is now very big. You surprised me in your last letter. Do you mean that you don't know all my mother's names? She is called Njoki but as you know that means being born again. So in the light of this, my mother has two names: *Njoki, and Wamũingĩ. Very many friends of ours have been coming to see the baby.* We miss you a great deal but we hope one day we shall be able to eat, laugh, discuss matters that concern us, and live together.
>
> *As you can see I have decided to write a rather long letter since unless things are relaxed we may not be able to see each other for a long time to come.* So what I am now most concerned with are the exact reasons for your detention. *When you were detained, we only gathered from the local and the international press that you are a political prisoner. I hope that you are being treated like a political prisoner. What gives me courage is because I know you are there not because of any crime you have committed. What gives me strength is my knowledge that you are not a criminal.*

I hope you received the books and the money I sent through Mr. Muhindi. Some books were returned to me but that is all right, I understand.

I have sent a pair of sandals and two pairs of underwear.
Hoping to read from you soon.
Mrs. Zirimu sends her greetings.

Salamia Wengine,
NYAMBURA

Nyambura's previous letters had been very brief, business-like. I could of course guess the source of their rigidity and hesitancy. She didn't want to give anything that might conceivably be used against me. But this last letter was relaxed and informative, and had even ventured into political questioning—and so soon after the visit that never was!

From the letter, I deconstructed the message. Njoki, born again as Wamũingĩ, belonged to the people. By extension, this was true of the other children. I should not worry about them in isolation from all the other children and families in Kenya. By alluding to the local and international press, she confirmed what I had learned from hints and oblique comments by the guards: my detention and imprisonment had raised some national and international concern. By expressing the hope that I was being treated like a political prisoner, she was saying that I should insist on my rights as a political prisoner.

The letter considerably buoyed up my spirits. I showed it to other political prisoners. Thairũ wa Mũthĩga commented, "It is good to have a politically conscious wife!" I couldn't help saying, "Amen." She may not have been politically conscious, but she had started asking questions. Those outside the barbed wire and the stone walls must ask questions and demand answers. It's the only way to defeat the culture of fear and silence. If a community of millions were to ask questions and demand answers, who would deny them?

Nyambura's letter had freed me from a certain fear. I was now psychologically and emotionally ready for the never-ending struggle with the stony dragon. I went back to cell 16, went back to Warĩnga and continued writing my novel with renewed vigor. On toilet paper.

Perhaps Njoki would one day read it and say that at least her father was ready to join all the Wamũingĩs of modern Kenya to say no to the culture of fear and silence, no to exploitation, oppression, and imperialist control of Kenya, to end that which so many, from Koitalel to Kĩmathi, had died fighting. Yes, she might tell her friends that her father had said *no* to the repressive stifling culture of parasites in paradise.

7

Meditations

Life in prison is not all endless confrontations and "profound" meditations on history. It is basically a cliché: dull, mundane, downright monotonous, repetitious, torturous in its intended animal rhythm of eating, defecating, sleeping, eating, defecating, sleeping. It is the rhythm of animals in a cage waiting for slaughter or escape from slaughter at a date not of their own fixing.

* * *

It has, though, its surface joys on deep sorrows: laughter —sometimes very genuine and spontaneous—on hidden tears; petty quarrels and friendships in a community of lonely strangers; distinctions of nationality and class in a community facing a single enemy; petty debating points that open new wounds on old ones that have not yet healed; gibes and innuendos that remain burning in the brain like salt on an incurable wound, among people who know that their survival depends on *not* tearing one another down as intended and encouraged by their captors; moments of genuinely revealing dialogues against the knowledge that this is leading nowhere; dreams against the background of the long, continuous nightmare that is prison itself. It's the dream that makes survival possible.

* * *

I seek comfort in José Martí: good is the earth, existence is holy, and in suffering itself, new reasons are found for living.

* * *

On arrival at Kamĩtĩ, I am received by a prison superintendent in a greenish long-sleeved shirt and khaki trousers, who ushers me into the chief guard's office. Beside him is a fat guard in khaki shorts and a green shirt. . . . The superintendent takes down all the details—name, profession, social habits ("Do you smoke or drink?"), religion ("None? Really?"), location, district. He assigns me a number, K6,77, in exchange for my name. The number means the sixth to be detained in Kamĩtĩ in the year 1977. The superintendent is young, with a business-like efficiency, but he is very polite. I had not in my mind associated prison service with youth, people with a future, and it now looks to me as if the young superintendent has strayed into the place, a stranger. But then I recall that two of my class of fifty-eight in Alliance High School opted for prison service. Business over, he raises his head—he has been sitting, and I have been standing—and says, "I have read all your books. I was planning to come to see *Ngaahika Ndeenda*. Then I read in the papers about the ban. Tell me, why really did they bring you to this place?" I say to myself, *Here now begins the long-awaited interrogation.* But his voice sounds sincere.

"I don't know," I tell him, adding, "but it could be because of *Ngaahika Ndeenda*."

"What's wrong with the play? What was it about?"

"Our history. The lives of peasants and workers."

"What's wrong with that?"

"I don't know!"

"No, there must have been something else," he says, as if he is talking to himself.

Then he suddenly shoots a question that is also a statement of his lingering doubts:

"Tell me the truth. Was the play really being acted by workers and peasants?"

"Yes. They all came from Kamīrīthū village!"

* * *

As I am led into cell 16, literally opposite the chief warder's office, I keep on wondering if I will be the sole occupant of this doleful place, presided over by a youthful-looking superintendent and a jelly-fleshed warder. No other human sight, no sound. Amid sepulchral silence, the warder ushers me into my new residence, and he locks the door from the outside. He then stuffs a piece of blanket into the bars on my door so that I cannot see anybody on the outside and nobody from outside the door can see me. Then suddenly the sepulchral silence is broken with wild shouts—"It's Ngũgĩ! It's wa Thiong'o!"—in Gĩkũyũ and Kiswahili. "Wĩyũmĩrĩrie! Jikaze! Gũtirĩ wa Iregi ũtũire!" continue the shouts.

It's the other political prisoners. They had been locked in their cells to free the warders to impose a state-of-emergency–type curfew in and around the prison. But the political prisoners had been peering through the iron-barred openings on the doors of their cells and some had witnessed my coming. It was Koigi wa Wamwere who, on recognizing me, started the shouts of regretful welcome. But this I don't now know and the voices, suddenly coming from the erstwhile silent walls, sound eerie.

Later, the political prisoners are let out in groups. They remove the piece of blanket covering the bars, they crowd around my door, and they ask me many questions all at once. But one question stands out above the others:

"Is it true that *Ngaahika Ndeenda* was acted by peasants and workers?"

* * *

I am secretly thrilled by the knowledge that the Kamĩrĩthũ Community effort had already broken through the walls of Kamĩtĩ Prison to give hope to political prisoners, who before had never heard of Kamĩrĩthũ.

* * *

Yes, *Ngaahika Ndeenda* has preceded me in prison. Throughout my stay, I'll get more inquiries about it. One comes from a warder of Kalenjin nationality who tells me the play was read and translated to him by his Mũgĩkũyũ friend who worked at a coffee plantation around Kĩambu. He tells me about the play and recounts the plot and mentions the names of several characters.

"I hope that I will one day be able to see a performance of the play," he says wistfully.

He is voicing the hope of many Kenyans, and it feels good. Truth, a peasant once told me, is like a mole. You can cover its hole, but it will still reappear in another place!

* * *

The welcome I receive from the other political prisoners is touching. Wasonga Sijeyo gives me a comb and a pair of tire sandals. Martin Shikuku gives me a handmade cell calendar. Gĩkonyo wa Rũkũngũ, the same. Adam Mathenge, a *kũngũrũ* uniform. Koigi wa Wamwere, a Biro pen. Gĩcerũ wa Njaũ, a pencil. Thairũ wa Mũthĩga, a Biro pen. Mũhoro wa Mũthoga, some writing paper with the prison letterhead. Later the pens and pencils will be confiscated, but the gesture to my intellectual needs is moving. Ali Dubat Fidhow, Hadji Dagane Galal, Hadji Mahat Kuno Roble, Ibrahim Ali Omer, Mzee Duale Roble Hussein—they all try to find something to give as a gesture of goodwill and solidarity. There's a fellowship that develops among people in adversity that's very human and gives glimpses of what human beings could become if they could unite against the enemy of humanity: social cannibalism.

* * *

In 1963 I opened a short story, "The Mubenzi Tribesman," with this sentence: "The thing that one remembers most about prison is the smell: the smell of shit and urine; the smell of human sweat and breath." This was fairly accurate for a young imagination. Prison has its own peculiar smell: a permanent pall of perpetually polluted air. On arrival at Kamĩtĩ, the smell hits me in the face, it descends on me, it presses me down, it courses down my nostrils and throat, I am gasping for breath, and I am really scared of an attack of asthma.

The smell of unsugared, unsalted, uncooked porridge is

another. It is nauseating. I feel like vomiting. Was I a Mubenzi tribesman after all?

Mathenge gives me a share of his own prescription of sugar to ease me into the habit of eating *unga* for all seasons. Yes, it's true: sugar, soup of boiled beans without fat or onions, what we called *makerũro ma mboco*, milk, tea, and rice are medicines given only on the orders of the prison doctor! Luckily I have never been choosy about what I eat.

There is also the smell of the warders and even that of the other political prisoners, and inwardly I am recoiling from the contact. Do they also feel the smell of the outsider? Is this how animals detect strangers in their midst?

Later I stop smelling all the smells. No matter how I sniff now, I don't sense the smell. Did I earlier imagine it?

And suddenly I realize that I am part of prison life. I am part of the life of the caged. Perhaps one does not remember the smell after all. To adjust is human. But not to accept evil.

* * *

Or perhaps it is the civilian clothes (on top of my forced segregation) that separate us. I look hard at the other prisoners in their tire sandals and their white *kũngũrũs* of collarless shirts and tight pants that match one's buttocks and narrowing thighs to the knee. I watch how they circle one another aimlessly, how they walk to and fro within the same walls, and the image of madmen in a lunatic asylum, with their erratic aimless wanderings and gestures, steals into my mind.

Later, when I get into my own *kũngũrũ* white uniform and discard the civilian outfit, I feel like one of them. The clothes, as the popular Gĩkũyũ musician Joseph Kamarũ would say, have made us all equal. After a time, I begin to feel "natural" in them. I even begin to see huge differences between the immaculately clean *kūngūrūs* and the dirty ones (before they all appeared of the same hue) and even to distinguish between the various cuts, really very minute differences, but there all the same.

When my internal segregation is over, I join in the same erratic, aimless circles and wanderings, going everywhere and nowhere. The compound is too tiny to give anybody the feel of a purposeful walk or even the illusion of one. I am now one of the inmates of this once famed lunatic asylum.

It is not a joke, really. The compound used to be for mentally deranged convicts before it was put to better use as a cage for the "politically deranged." In a sense, we are truly mad. Imagine anyone questioning the morality of man-cat-man in a state of man-eaters? Imagine anyone questioning the ethic of eating human flesh and drinking human blood when Western bourgeois civilization—God-given, universal, and final in its American form—has taught its worshippers that social cannibalism is the highest good! Madness, after all, is relative. It depends on who is calling whom mad. In a state of madmen, anybody who is not mad is mad. This is the truth in Chekhov's literary masterpiece, "Ward No. 6."

However, human sanity will never be drowned in a pool of inhuman madness, for if a country has a class of man-eaters, then it has to have men to be eaten, and will these victims of others' greed always let themselves and their kind be eaten up forever? The fact is that the objects of social cannibalism will never accept the morality of man-eaters as the all-time universal morality, not even if it comes dressed in draperies marked

Free World, Democracy, Christendom, Western Civilization, Global modernity, and other dazzling, platitudinous labels.

* * *

I arrive in Kamĩtĩ on Saturday, December 31, 1977. On January 13, 1978, four new political prisoners are brought in—Ahmed Shurie Abdi, Mohamed Nurie Hanshi, Mohamed Abdilie Hadow, and Mohamed Dahir Digale—all Kenyans of Somali nationality. Three days later, on January 16, the ex–senior chief of Garissa, Sugow Ahmed Adan, also of Somali nationality, is brought in.

I now feel like an old boy in relation to the newcomers. But a thought keeps on nagging at me. Could there have been more arrests and detentions in Limuru? I ask some of the newcomers, but they can't recollect any such news. There is nobody else to ask. Not now, anyway.

* * *

My first contact with—or shall I say the first communication from—the outside world is a formal note from our family and childhood friend, lawyer Ndere wa Njũgi. It is a simple, to-the-point kind of letter sent through the office of the president and brought by hand by a police officer.

> Greetings from Nyambura Ngũgĩ and the family. The purpose of writing this letter is to request you to sign a few blank cheques which Nyambura could use to draw money when need arises. You took your cheque book with you.
>
> Everything is okay.

It is signed by Nyambura and the lawyer. I know their signatures, and they look authentic. The chief warder gives me back
my checkbook—everything, including my driver's license and
a few shillings, had been signed in and kept under lock and
key—and I sit down and sign all the leaves.

I study the letter. It is typed on plain paper—without a letterhead. It is dated January 10. The signatures are in ink. And
they still look authentic. So Nyambura has already been in
touch with the lawyer? There was a village teacher who once
read to my Standard Four class at Manguū (and later to the
school assembly of students and parents) a composition I had
written in the Gīkūyū language. "This is how to write," he told
them. But he became almost mad with anger when years later he
heard that I had opted to study English—mere words—instead
of one of the more substantial professional courses like engineering, medicine, or law. "Really, why don't you take law?"

Now I recall all this as I keep fingering the letter. If I had
taken law or medicine or engineering or architecture, instead
of being drawn to mere words, would I be in Kamītī today?

Why not? Today more and more professionals are realizing that their sciences, which should serve people—for really,
medicine, science, and technology were developed by working people to free themselves from the capricious tyranny of
nature—are benefiting only the plutocratic class instead of
the masses. Moneyless needs get indifference; moneyed greed
makes all the difference. Discoveries and inventions, which
are collective and social in origin, end up as private property.

A contented, pipe-smoking fellow sits on another's back.
Medicine, science, and technology, instead of going to the aid
of him (and her) whose back is sat upon, rush to the aid of the

fellow in the three-piece suit to ensure his health and strength so he can continue to ride on the backs of the others. Armaments go to protect the moneycrats against any challenges to the status quo. The law rushes to protect the property that the pipe-smoking fellow has stolen from those he rides.

Some Kenyan professionals are beginning to see the utter immorality of that structure and their own roles in servicing it. At the very least, they question and reject the comprador bourgeois ethic, which declares on roofs and mountaintops that the foreign is progress; the national is backward; deride the national.

Maybe even if I had taken law or medicine or engineering, I would have ended up in Kamĩtĩ, for probably I would at one time have been tempted to shout, "Foreign capital, go home!"

Well, I chose words. And now I am studying words asking me to sign a few checks to enable Nyambura to withdraw money as need arises. When I am released, I will learn that the checkbook was Nyambura's first assurance that I had not been "sent to Ngong."[1]

Words? What counts is the reality they reflect.

* * *

In the period of my internal segregation, I keep on studying the other political prisoners, and I am amazed to find that the different groups span the entire history of postindependence upheavals. I am not here talking about whether they were involved in the upheavals, which the ruling party saw as a challenge to its monopoly of power. I am not even concerned as to whether that challenge was real or imagined, but the excuses for detaining them can definitely be associated with the several major crises in Kenya's period of independence. But the fact that the prisoners span many communities, social classes, and professions and cover the entire postcolonial history, from independence to the ban on Kamĩrĩthũ, speaks of continuous struggle.

There was another side to my detention: the growing anti-imperialist consciousness among peasants, workers, university lecturers, and students, and I was the sacrificial lamb!

Thought for despair? No! I am part of a living history of struggle. And without struggle, there is no movement, there is no life.

* * *

The thought is not original—I once read it in William Blake: without contraries there is no progression; attraction and repulsion, reason and energy, love and hate, are necessary to human existence. And later in Hegel: contradiction is the root of all movement and all life, and only insofar as a thing incorporates a contradiction is it mobile, does it possess impulse and activity. But it is true!

* * *

The warders talk of him with awe; the political prisoners, with a mixture of bitterness, contempt, and hatred. He is Edward P. Lokopoyet, the senior superintendent of prisons in charge of Kamĩtĩ Prison, and hence the detention block. Gradually I begin to comprehend the magnitude of this man's relentless tyranny over the political prisoners, as narrated.

For over two years, this officer has waged a war to break the political prisoners en masse physically and mentally. He has had them locked up in the cells for twenty-three hours a day for two consecutive years, a complete negation of every single prison rule and regulation. He might order uncooked food to be brought to them; food with bits of grass and sand thrown in; ugali cooked in warm water; beans and yellow vegetables enriched with worms and other insects; and whenever he comes into the compound (rare!), it is to reprimand political prisoners for not showing proper respect to oppressive authority. Tall, strong, dark, and smooth faced, he struts about the compound, the very embodiment of all the written and unwritten oppressive laws of Kenya. He is himself the law. He is the mini-god, and he is genuinely puzzled why these political pariahs do not see this and act accordingly. So he daily redoubles and trebles and quadruples the previous efforts to make them see the light and understand who he is and which forces in society he represents. It was during his reign that the chaining of political prisoners was started. It was during his sovereignty over Kamĩtĩ that the radio and newspapers were denied to prisoners.

These actions have only generated a huge antagonism from the political prisoners, who do not mince words in his presence. They keep on reminding him about the inevitability of change. He once lectured a political prisoner for taking the initiative of extending a hand to him in greeting. He, the political prisoner, should have waited to be greeted. The humiliating reprimand backfires. Now, whenever he himself takes out his hand to greet the political prisoners, they turn their heads the other way so that his hand is left hanging in the air.

The political prisoners decide to write a collective memorandum of protest against the intolerable conditions. Their letter, dated January 1977, is addressed to Mr. Mūhīndī Mūnene, the security officer in charge of the political prisoners, through Justice Hancox, the chairman of the Political Prisoners Review Tribunal:

> The inhuman and difficult conditions to which we are subjected now are an extreme hazard to the maintenance of our minimum physical and mental health, health that is already strained by its efforts to survive under the basic Detention conditions, conditions that are abnormal to human living. Certain that the weight and roughness of these conditions are severely and cruelly bruising our physical and mental health, we are appealing to you to uplift these conditions now before they exact from our health the high toll of a conspicuous and irreparable damage. In appealing to you to free us from these conditions, we also appeal to you against the wisdom of thinking that damage upon physical and mental health must stick out a mile to count. Sir, by the time it sticks out a mile, it will no longer be damage but destruction and we hope and pray that this is not what the future holds in store for us.

But only a few eventually sign it; Major L.B. Mwanzia, Adamu Mathenge Wangombe, Ongongi Were, Gīcerū wa Njaū, Koigi wa Wamwere, Thairū wa Mūthīga. And one of those signing it, Major Mwanzia, is immediately transferred to Shimo La Tewa prison in Mombasa.

But the mutual hatred, contempt, and antagonism continue. The letter is not answered. And nothing is done about their grievances about confinement, food, medication, mail, visits, handcuffs, radio, and newspapers.

Gradually the antagonism begins to tell on him. His rare visits become even rarer. Now he sneaks in, then quickly runs out as if safari ants were crawling all over the tiny compound. This however makes him even more repressive. He is incapable of seeing that there could be greatness in recognition of one's mistakes and failures. Now he uses his juniors to execute what he has mapped out in the office.

Because he himself is hardly there in the compound, the antagonism between him and the political prisoners works out, in practice, as an antagonism between the guards and the political prisoners. Abusive language, innuendos, gibes, outright denunciation: the tension building up could literally be cut with an electric saw, and everybody is sure that sooner or later violence will erupt. At one time, so I am told, a more sensitive warder breaks down and weeps: "Some of us are really sorry about all this. Please understand that we are only carrying out orders. If I should lose my job, what will my children eat, where will they get their clothes and school fees? Where will they sleep?"

The other political prisoners tell me that the slight relaxation I see in the compound is because the ordinary guards have become bored and tired of carrying out the tyrannical commands of the prison sovereign. Of course, I do not see any relaxation, big or small. But if the harsh conditions of my three-week stay are any kind of relaxation, then their last two years were actual hell.

Wasonga Sijeyo, the longest resident at the compound, confirms this: "I was in colonial detention for five years. And now, after Independence, I have also been in this compound for nine years. But these last two years have been the worst of all the previous twelve years!"

* * *

This Edward P. steals into my cell one morning. He times the visit when all the other political prisoners are in their cells. He lectures me for an hour on the virtues of total submission. "Don't copy some of these other political prisoners. Did you know any before you came here? Never mind. I will tell you the truth. They don't really want to go home. Let me tell you, if you behave yourself, who knows, you might go home any day. Some political prisoners have gone home after only two or three weeks. Others, as you can see, have been here for nine years. It is all up to you." He tries out the divisive politics of flattery and threats. "You see, you are the most highly educated person—well, I should say the only educated person, for what education have these others? Some are not even politicians—and so if anything that requires brains happens here, it will be blamed on you." As he is about to leave, he says, "And remember, don't attempt to write any poems here. Not unless I have given you permission. And even then I must see the poems and approve!"

He walks out*. The arrogance of power. The confidence of ignorance. And suddenly I know that I have to write, I must write. My main problem will be finding ways and means of hiding the written notes. And if caught, well, I get caught!

---

*To be fair to Edward Lokopoyet, I am reporting what the others told me about his deeds prior to my encounter with him. He was never rude to me, personally, but of course I also suffered under the atmosphere he had created.

Wrote William Blake in *The Marriage of Heaven and Hell*:

The prophets Isaiah and Ezekiel dined with me, and I asked them how they dared so roundly to assert that God spoke to them; and whether they did not think at the time that they would be misunderstood, & so be the cause of imposition.

Isaiah answer'd: "I saw no God, nor heard any, in a finite organical perception; but my senses discover'd the infinite in every thing, and as I was then perswaded, & remained confirm'd; that the voice of honest indignation is the voice of God, I cared not for consequences but wrote.

* * *

The Military Man. He has been here for three years. He keeps to himself; he hardly came to my door to say hallo, but the moment my internal segregation ends, he befriends me. This intensifies after we discover we both like chess—chess and checkers are some of the few games allowed. Checkers is the more popular. Some of the prisoners breathe and swear by it, but Military Man looks down upon it. He was used to a daily chess company of another military officer; the two used to play it with gripping intensity as if they were indeed commanding armies in a battlefield. Besides their military past, chess was what set them apart. Then the officer was transferred to Shimo La Tewa prison. So between the departure of the officer and my arrival on the scene, he has had nobody to play chess with, for Military Man does not deign to teach the others. Chess becomes the special knowledge that he possesses and the others, civilians, don't. But I am a little different; being a professor and a writer compensate for my lack of a military background. Plus, I already know how to play chess, and he notices, after a few checkmates, that I am able to outmaneuver him on the chessboard.

Initially, some of the others express an interest and the desire to learn, and I teach them the names of the pieces and their moves, much to the chagrin of Military Man, who likes it that it is a game known to a few, but he is not upset for long, for the moment the others discover that chess is not like checkers but calls for more concentration, they abandon it one by one, and in the end, only Military Man and I are left to it, confirming to the Military Man his view that chess calls for superior minds. At first, the others, even when they do not play, would watch Military Man and me play, but after a time, they don't even stop at our sessions. Later I learn the rumor that has driven them away. A few even try to discourage me, for my own sanity. Chess and the concentration it calls for, even watching it, can make one crazy, and they think Military Man is a little crazed.

* * *

I don't care. He regales me with stories, not so much of his actual military experience, but of the aura that surrounds it. He hints that he had indeed been privy to a military plot to overthrow the Kenyatta regime, and sometimes he himself was somehow in the thick of it, but he never divulges details of what, who, when, where, and how. But the very lack of details and his mysterious looks make his involvement seem bigger than he was letting on. The more I listened, the more extraordinary his hints and claims became. Sometimes he would tell me, without details, that he had trained with the PLO, that he had even met with Arafat. He talked about some of the leading figures in the organization. Just before my incarceration, there had been news of the arrest of two Palestinians at Nairobi airport. He swore me to secrecy; then he divulged the secret. They had been sent by the top PLO leadership to rescue him from Kamĩtĩ prison. Despite the setback, the plans to spring him from prison were still afoot. His stories make him look larger than life, although this was in contrast to his haggard prisoner bearing.

* * *

Koigi takes me aside one day, and he tells me word for word the stories the Military Man must have been telling me. What? Had he been listening? No, it was because he and others had been recipients of those stories before.

* * *

It turns out, according to Koigi, that Military Man has never been in military service, but he happened to be social friends with some in the military later arrested and detained without trial for being suspected of plotting a coup. The real military officer—the chess partner who came before me—had told on him. He is a victim of social contact; at any rate he was never in the military. But since his imprisonment without trial, he has internalized the military thing, and in his mind he was really in the military. What about his seemingly good knowledge of the PLO and even naming some of the leaders and other actors in the Middle East? Well, there was a period, before my time, when they were allowed newspapers, and the Military Man had an incredible memory that retained all the details. He had a way of inserting himself in the stories in a manner that seemed convincing, except that logic dictated the contrary. Plus, the real military officer, who had been transferred, had told them the truth. I became even more interested in his fiction.

* * *

He lived in a fantasy in which brave men would eventually rescue him, and when angry with the prison officials, he would hint at some kind of retribution. Whatever it is, the fantasy, I suppose, keeps hope alive . . . hope . . . and one needs hope in this hopeless place.

Does it matter how one gets it, whether from religious faith or in the rightness of one's political beliefs? Or in the stories of a Military Man sustained by dreams of a giant dramatic rescue?

* * *

I will try a diary of life in prison. I'll record everything that happens: what I see, touch, smell, hear, and think. But no matter how hard I try, no words will form on paper. I was never one for writing diaries and records, and whenever in the past I have tried it—at Manguū and Kīnyogori primary schools, at Alliance High School, at Makerere and Leeds universities—I have always had to give it up after one or two false starts. I am too close to the events for me to see them clearly or to immediately make out what's happening to me.

Besides that, I find that here at Kamīti, in a certain sense, everything is so very ordinary—well, worse than ordinary, for

time here is sluggish, space is narrow, and any action is a repetition of similar nonactions—that I have nothing outstand-
ing to record. Yesterday as today: Is that enough for a diary?

For similar reasons, I have never tried to write an
autobiography—even when publishers have requested it—for
my life has been ordinary, average really, and it would bore me
to death. No, I'll let impressions form in my mind until they
accumulate into a composite picture.

But I could write about premonitions, wish fulfilments,
because these have always struck me as oddly inexplicable.
My very first piece of writing to be published, in the *Alliance
High School Magazine*, was based on a belief we used to have
as children, that if you strongly desired your aunt, whom you
had not seen in a long time, to come home, you could actually
make her appear by dipping your head in a black pot and whis-
pering to her. I think I did that once. And she came home. In
the story, when I try to demonstrate my occult powers, the
results are negative.

Many critics have pointed out the parallels between my
own arrest and detention and similar but fictional events in
the opening and closing chapters of my novel *Petals of Blood*.
It opens with the arrest of a progressive worker—he is deceived
into believing that he is wanted at the police station for a few
questions—and it closes with his eventual detention and
imprisonment on suspicion of being a communist at heart.

Or one Sunday a week before my arrest, and for the first time
in my life, I drove past the outer gates of Kamĩtĩ Prison, lin-
gered there for a few seconds wondering what it really looked
like inside, before continuing my slow drive to a friend's house
at Kahawa. I was there for only a few seconds. Suddenly I felt

sad and tired. "You know," I told him as we looked at books in his study, "I feel as if I am living on borrowed time."

But what I really want to write about is the day, in fact the Wednesday before my arrest, when the whole Limuru countryside seemed the most glorious landscape I had ever seen. Madly, I drove past Kikuyu, past Dagoretti Market, past Karen and on to Ngong Hills. The day was very clear, the sky a brilliant blue, and the landscape a luscious green. Down below was the whole expanse of Maasailand and the Rift Valley. To my left, facing Nairobi, I could see a very clear outline of Mount Kenya with its snowcaps against the blue sky. The same for Kilimambogo . . . and the Akamba mountain ranges beyond Athi River town. . . . Everything seemed to grow beautiful and clear under a skin-warming sunshine. "I have never seen Kenya like this," I told my companion. Let's go back to Limuru via Gĩthũngũri.

I try to scribble something about this experience, and it sounds unreal, sentimental, and I am unable to write more than two lines. But throughout my forced stay at Kamĩtĩ, unable to see any green landscape, any contours of valleys and hills and mountains, I continue remembering the vision of that Wednesday with a kind of gratitude.

* * *

My argument with the reverend keeps on coming back to me. I grew up with the Bible, mostly the Old Testament, and most of the characters—Abraham, Isaac, David, Joseph—were my early companions in my village. This was because when I learned to read and write, the only book readily available was the Gĩkũyũ language Old Testament. I enjoyed some magical moments: Jonah surviving three days in the belly of a fish; Shadrach, Meshach, and Abednego surviving fiery flames. It's the survival part that's most appealing.

* * *

But some sections of the New Testament, as well: the Sermon on the Mount, John the Baptist surviving his sojourn in the wilderness on honey and wild berries. The devil tempted him to quit? The devil once even dared tempt Jesus. They had wrestled with the devil, and emerged stronger from the contest. Did the reverend come to tempt me?

* * *

I resent the fact that they cannot tell us a thing about the outside, not even about rain or wind or sunshine. Birds fly far above the walls of the prison. I wish they could lend me their wings, just for a day. What would I do with them? Visit my family, my village, but also what? Oh yes, go to all the houses and offices of those in power, making mischief, or land at caves where they're planning corruption, and scatter their plates and knives, practical jokes. And then back. No, I won't come back, I will not come back to this confinement. But the fun is in going and coming back, at will, and enjoying their foolishness in thinking they can confine me within their man-made walls. But this—going and coming—is what I do night and day. I visit my family. I walk the streets. My imagination is my wings of glory.

* * *

A novel. That's what I must do. In Gĩkũyũ. That would be fun, writing a novel in the language that made them bring me here. Yes. Combine fun with fight and flight. But no story would form.

* * *

There was a time when I visited Vihiga and western Kenya. I fly back there, and I see the rocks, the Napoléon rocks, and I remember I had wanted to write a story about it. I had even started it? But I cannot remember the plot. All I recall was that there was a devil in it.

* * *

Kim Chi Ha's poem "The Five Bandits" tells the story of a contest of skills in theft among a business tycoon (whose custom-made suit is tailored of banknotes), a politician, a bureaucrat, a general, and a government minister. I read it from *The Cry of the People*, a book of his poems I picked up in a bookshop in Tokyo. I have been teaching it at the University of Nairobi, and it goes down very well. I can visualize a similar competition among those who brought me here.

* * *

I need paper. Pen. Writing material. The warders have plenty. I want to write something, I tell them, hinting it might even be a confession; the older political prisoners had told me of the trick. It always works, they had told me, because that's what they want us to do, confess, and indeed the chief warder readily complies. A ballpoint, but only a few sheets. Never mind. I can supplement that with, well, toilet paper. Good. The idea eludes me.

[Ndi](2)
maake, o mũũndũ akoo-
naga ta aarekia ũrĩa
ũngĩ ta we aangĩũrĩra
nduma-inĩ ĩyo ya ũtheri
wa Nguruunga-inĩ ya
Ilmorog.

Macaria mokĩria nĩ
aataangagwo nĩ mee-
ciiria maingĩ ũũ ati
ndaahotaga kũrũmĩrĩ-
ra mĩario ya njũngwa-
inĩ. O na ndaahotaga
kũrũkĩrĩria rĩĩciiria
rĩmwe, Rĩmwe rĩokaga,
rĩgathũitha hamiini, te
rĩgacooka rĩgathii ka-
ruwena-inĩ; rĩingĩ rĩgoo
ka rĩkarũngarũnga

But soon another idea steals into my sleep. It begins to form a shape. Around a competition among wealthy robbers. Probably not so original, remember Kim Chi Ha? But it strongly appeals to me.

* * *

Jesus and the devil come back to my mind.

* * *

I still wrestle with my arguments with the reverend. The idea that it was the devil and not Christ who should have been executed on the cross plays in my mind. Jesus was an opponent of Roman imperialism, a proponent of the kingdom of the least among us, a visionary who saw the poor, among whom he walked, as inheriting the earth. The devil was an ally of Roman imperialism and its oppressive practices, a self-serving criminal whose followers, exploiters of the poor, have as much chance of entering heaven as a camel through the eye of the needle. A competition of modern robbers organized by the devil. But the story refuses to form.

* * *

Chief Mohamed Nurie tells me fantastic Somali folklore of heroic exploits by Kabaalaf and Egal Shidad. With little variations of word and place, they are like those of Hare and Abunuwasi.

Hadji Dagan tells me about the real-life anti-imperialist military and literary exploits of Sayyid Mohammed Abdullah Hassan, the great African patriot whose history Kenya shares with Somalia. Does he belong to Kenya or Somalia?

Kenya, Ethiopia, and Somalia share common borders, some common nationalities, and hence some common history. The united peoples' socialist states of Kenya, Ethiopia, and Somalia, a union freely entered by the peoples of the three territories, holds a great future because of the past the three peoples share.

Idle thoughts: to whom would the imperialist powers sell the obsolete products of their war industries?

* * *

The trouble with you educated people is that you despise your languages. You don't like talking to ordinary people. But what use is your education if it cannot be shared with your own people? Let me tell you. You may possess all the book education in the world, but it's we, ordinary people in tattered clothes with bare feet and blistered hands, who have the real knowledge of things. If I was to wear a suit today, you would see me a different person, but it would not mean that I had suddenly acquired more knowledge and wisdom than I had when wearing tattered clothes. Have you seen any European calling himself Mutiso, Kamau, Onyango, Kiplagat, or Simiyu? Have you seen Europeans abandoning their languages and bothering about our languages? Let me tell you something else. Yes, I may not have book knowledge, but even a child can give you a word that might benefit you. You people, even if you follow Europeans to the grave, they will never never let you really know their languages. They will never—and mark my words, don't look down upon a drop of rain—Europeans will never let you into the secrets held by their languages. . . . What do you then become? Their slaves!

It is an ordinary Mũgĩkũyũ warder talking to me, no, actu-

ally lecturing me, for I am speechless with disbelief. Is he trying to trap me into something indiscreet, anything? Does he
know what he's talking about? Doesn't he know that I'm here
precisely because of trying to communicate with peasants and
workers—ordinary people, as he calls them?

But there is a kind of frank bitterness in his voice that
shows much sincerity in his holding me and my "class"
responsible for the cultural plight of Kenya. I think he is
utterly unconscious of the fact that what he is saying, were
he to try and put it into practice, could land him in this very
detention block.

I say he is genuine in his utter lack of consciousness of the
heretical nature of his position on culture, because he is one of
the few warders who seem to have been completely cowed by
prison and authority. If you asked him about the weather outside, he would shrink back in fear, pleading: "Please don't play
fire with my job. It is where I get daily flour for my children."
So in saying this to me, it is probably because he thinks it a
safe subject. Languages, culture, education? Who cares? I am
content just to listen to his monologue.

What have Europeans done to you people that you follow
them like dogs their master? What have they done to you that
you despise your own tongues and your own country?

I cannot answer him. I am itching to tell him about the
Kamĩrĩĩthũ experiment, but I know that if I so much as mention the name Kamĩrĩĩthũ, he will freeze in terror, change the
subject, and move away from the door of cell 16. But his talk
has stung me in ways that he will never know.

That night I sit at the desk and start the story of Warĩnga
in the Gĩkũyũ language. I don't know how, but the idea of a

competition of robbers organized by the devil becomes central to Warīnga's adventures. It flows just like that, and for the first time since my incarceration, I feel transports of joy. That which I have always toyed with but feared—writing a novel in Gĩkũyũ—is happening before my own eyes, and I have government toilet paper for writing material and a government-paid guard as a consultant. I am ever willing to learn. In prison, more so.

* * *

Throughout my stay in Kamĩtĩ, and looking at all the Kenyan nationalities represented in this compound, I note one dominant tendency. While in ordinary social talks, petty reminiscences, and occasional jokes and family problems, people tend to retreat into their own nationalities, when it comes to serious issues, confrontation with authority, demands for our rights and justice, the walls of nationality break asunder and people group around given positions vis-à-vis the issues. Even when it comes to the interpretation of Kenyan history and Kenya's future, people tend to group around definite ideological positions.

I have seen a similar tendency among the warders of different nationalities. There are times when they express the bitterness of an oppressed, exploited class and talk to us as if they see in us just members of an exploiting, oppressing propertied class who have only temporarily fallen from grace and out of favor with other brothers-in-plunder.

* * *

Strange how a place acquires its own personality, history, even culture and special vocabulary. All those who have been in this compound have become part of the spirit of our history as political prisoners. Those of us who are new can never hear enough about the personalities, characters, anecdotes, exploits, words, songs, and sayings of those who were here before us and have now left. Cyrus Jamaitta, Achieng Oneko, J.D. Kali, Ndhiwa, Mak'anyengo, Waweru Gĩthĩũngũri, and the renowned *mganga* (medicine man) Kajiwe, etc.—all these acquire legendary proportions in our imagination. Even some senior superintendents of prison (SSPs) and prison officers who have served in this block and have left, have become part of the block's history and legends. It's as if we are all part of an undeclared social fraternity.

* * *

If you were in prison for life or if you were shipwrecked on an island, what books would you like to have with you and why? That used to be a favorite question of literature teachers at Alliance High School and later at Makerere College. The normal response was to mention, not the books one would have liked to have—the situation envisaged by the question was anyway too remote even for imagination—but the novels or the volume of plays or poetry that one had studied in depth, on which one could do an adequate critical appreciation to earn one a good mark.

But here at Kamĩtĩ, the question is no longer academic, and when I receive news that my books have arrived, I tremble with excitement at the arrival of a package from home and with eagerness to know which books have been allowed through by the police and prison censors.

In Kamĩtĩ, there's no library of any sort. This is a great indictment of conditions in government prisons. The Bible and the Koran are the sole official library. A few political prisoners have had books sent them from home, and they have lent me some. I have particularly enjoyed reading Shaaban bin Robert's *Maisha yangu* (My Life) and *Masomo yenye adili* (Lessons with a Moral); Dickens's *A Tale of Two Cities*; René Fülöp-Miller's *Leaders, Dreamers, and Rebels*; John Abbott's *Life of Napoleon Bonaparte*; Kwame Kwei-Armah's *Fragments*; Aristotle's *Ethics*; and Dennis Brutus's *Letters to Martha*. Otherwise, the titles and authors available are too few and too limited in emotional and intellectual range. Therefore in asking for authors and titles from my home library, I have taken into account both my needs and those of the other political prisoners, so the list includes several authors and titles I have read and taught at university.

I am happy, though, for a prison reunion with Voltaire, Balzac, Molière, Zola, Flaubert, Tolstoy, Chekhov, Gorky, Sembène Ousmane, Shakespeare, Bertrand Russell, and Claude McKay, and to make new acquaintances like Elechi Amadi and Thomas Mann.

Suddenly I stop, shocked by those titles and authors that are barred by the censors. Books about British colonialism in Kenya are not allowed; hence W. McGregor Ross's *Kenya from Within*, a history discussing British colonial fascism in Kenya in the 1920s, has not come through.

Books about the Boer oppression of Africans in South Africa are not allowed through; hence Donald Woods's *Biko* has been returned to sender.

Books about slavery, racism, and political oppression in the heartland of imperialism, the USA, are not allowed; hence

Alex Haley's *Roots* has also been returned to sender. I now want to know more.

From the other political prisoners, I learn that any book discussing *socialism* (or simply with *socialism* in the title) is not allowed in, and of course any books bearing the names of Marx, Engels, Lenin, or Stalin, not to mention Mao Tsetung, are banned from detention. I am also told that Abdilatif Abdalla's book of poems titled *Sauti ya dhiki* (Voice of Agony), based on his experiences as a political prisoner at Kamītī, as well as my novel *Petals of Blood*, have been returned.

Now a few prison puzzles. Why has *Mwendwo nī Irī na Irīīri* (One Favored by Wealth and Honor) been returned? The title? The language?

Why has William Ochieng's book, *The Second Word: More Essays on Kenya History*, been returned? Most of the books by William Ochieng, which I had read before detention, were based on a neocolonial interpretation of Kenyan history. Could this book be different? Or was there another reason for banning it? The fact that he now teaches at Kenyatta University College? The fact that he once taught at Nairobi University, where I also used to teach?

But I am grateful for what has been allowed through, especially for Gorky's *Selected Short Stories* and *Selected Plays*. Truly beautiful is Gorky's story of Danko, who, when his people are trapped in a big, dark, and apparently impenetrable forest in their march toward liberation, courageously rips open his breast and tears out his heart and holds it high above his head to lift up their flagging faith. "It shone like the sun, even brighter than the sun, and the raging forest was subdued and lighted up by this torch, the torch of the great love for the people, and the darkness retreated before it."

Danko's story reminds me of one of Blake's proverbs: He whose face gives no light, shall never become a star.

Gorky has shown the way. Art should encourage people to bolder and higher resolves in all their struggles to free the human spirit from the twin manacles of oppressive nature and nurture.

* * *

J.M. Dent, publishers, have an interesting sentence in all the books that bear their imprint of Everyman's Library. The book is supposed to be telling the reader: "Everyman, I will go with thee, and be thy guide, In thy most need to go by thy side." The line is taken from a medieval English morality play. But it is Wasonga Sijeyo who makes me recall the line.

"Books," he tells me one day, "books have kept my mind alive. Without books, I don't know if I could have survived this long. If prison has taught me anything, it is a big respect for books. You know I never went to anybody's formal school. Not even once. All my education has been in the streets of struggle or else in concentration camps."

He is very widely read, with a keen, informed interest in geography, astronomy, philosophy, biology (especially the character and behavior of animals), world history, culture, literature, religion, and, of course, politics. His knowledge of the material culture of the Luo nationality is truly phenomenal, and I keep on urging him to write a book about it.

As I see him devouring Russell's three-volume autobiography, Tolstoy's *War and Peace*, and Balzac's *Père Goriot* and *Eugénie Grandet*, he symbolizes the kind of brilliance and genius pushed to the fore in periods of genuine people's struggles. The 1952–1962 armed struggle of the Kenya Land and Freedom Army (Mau Mau) was such a period in Kenya's history, and Wasonga Sijeyo was one of its direct products. I am sure, and I keep on telling him, that a story of his own life would be very instructive to Kenyan youth and he should write it down.

I wish, though, that I had asked for Gorky's three-volume autobiography, *My Childhood*, *My Apprenticeships*, and *My Universities*. I'm sure Wasonga Sijeyo would have readily recognized Gorky's universities.

* * *

However, no book or shelf of books can substitute for the book of life. The fascination people find in newspapers is precisely the illusion of daily participation in and a record of active life. Reading through a newspaper, one gets glimpses of a tapestry of life as it is being daily woven by actions of numerous men and women.

In prison detention, where people are not allowed newspapers or the radio, the thirst and hunger for news are sometimes unbearable in their torturous insistence.

Thus, gathering news at Kamĩtĩ is a psychological imperative, and the political prisoners have developed a fantastic instinct for nosing out and extracting news from reluctant warders. A political prisoner who goes out to the hospital or to meet his family must be hawkeyed. He must learn to tune and turn his ears with the deftness and alertness of a cat or a hare. Every word counts. Every building, vehicle, street, dress, and color of trees counts. When he returns to camp, each of these is discussed and analyzed from every possible angle till they yield all their secrets. A similar process, of course, takes place outside the prison, where radio and other media are so uninformative about the real events that people inevitably rely on inferences, deductions, and the grapevine. This is what is erroneously termed rumormongering by the rulers. But in prison, as outside, these inferences are often correct and help make sense of what's unfolding.

Sometimes a warder has gone out to buy, let's say, a toothbrush for a political prisoner. He might bring it wrapped in a piece of newspaper. Should he forget to remove it, then the piece of paper, however tiny, will be seized, and once again, every word, every line, will be discussed and analyzed until it too yields all the secrets, past and present.

One day, I get a dramatic illustration of news gathering at Kamĩtĩ. I am in cell 6. I feel down because after writing a whole chapter of my new novel without a problem, I have now come to a dead end. Every writer of imaginative literature knows the frustration and desperation that seize a person during such moments. It is naturally worse in prison.

Suddenly Mathenge, who keeps teasing me that he is the *original* Kamĩtĩ 6 because his number is K6,75 and mine is K6,77, bursts into my cell with a tiny piece of newspaper no larger than a few square inches. "Look at this," he shouts. "I collected it from the rubbish-bin outside. I saw a warder throw in some rubbish. I went and saw this, quickly picked it up and hid it before he could see me. It says something about Gachago and Muhuri [Jesse Mwangi Gachago and Godfrey Muhuri Muchiri, two prominent politicians at the time] and conviction, and oh, yes, look, there's a letter J . . . oh, wait, let the warders come on night duty."

At night two warders come. Then suddenly Mathenge calls out one by name:

"Hey! Have Gachago and Muhuri started their years on the other side?"

"You mean the two MPs? They started some time ago."

"How many years?"

"Five each. Plus a few strokes."

"What for?"

"Coffee, of course. Magendo. Corruption."

Then suddenly the warder realizes that he's talking to a political prisoner and he stops short.

"Who told you?"

"Never mind. Walls have voices."

Tomorrow Mathenge will use this information just gathered to get more information about where the two politicians are held, and within a week the whole story will be out, all from the guards' own mouths.

The news, though, has an unsettling effect on me. Magendo, corruption, smuggling ivory, gemstones, game-skins, coffee, corn, rice, sugar, *unga*, tea has been a way of life among the ruling circles in Kenya. Even the smallest child in a village could tell you the names of Big So-and-So, Tall So-and-So, Fat So-and-So, Moral So-and-So, Holy So-and-So, Upright So-and-So, who had camped at Chepkubwe[2] waiting for his tons of coffee, later transported to Mombasa under police escort. Why then pick on these two lawbreakers? Or were they just sacrificial lambs to propitiate an angry populace and buy time for a rotting, falling-apart system?

Capitalism itself is a system of unabashed theft and robbery. Thus theft, robbery, and corruption can never be wrong
under capitalism, because they are inherent in it. Well, they
are the structure. Without a systematic robbery of peasants
and workers, a robbery protected and sanctified by laws, law
courts, parliament, religion, armed forces, police, prisons, and
education, there is no capitalism. It is worse, the robbery, when
a country is under the higher capitalism of foreigners, which is
imperialism. How else explain the fact that in a mainly agri-
cultural country, peasants who farm often have to line up for
yellow corn from America and Britain after what they have
produced has been carted or sold or smuggled to those very
countries? Lenin once defined imperialism as the highest
stage of capitalism. Imperialism is the capitalistic robbery and
theft of a country's wealth, human and natural resources, by
foreigners aided, of course, by a few sell-out natives. Two MPs
put in the cooler for small offenses while the fat cats continue
profiteering unabated.

And suddenly I discover the hitherto elusive theme of
my prison novel. I grow literary wings. I am ready to fly. All
because of a piece of newspaper little larger than a square inch
retrieved from a trash bin by a fellow political prisoner!

* * *

Political prisoners have also learned to gather news from the
guards by reading their faces and group behavior. Certain
kinds of groupings by certain warders have come to mean that
some upheaval, good or bad for the political prisoners, has
happened outside the block. A certain kind of laughter from
the crueler guards has come to mean that something not to

the advantage of political prisoners has occurred, while a certain kind of sadness and fear on the same faces has invariably come to mean good news for us. This intuitive news-gathering style is inherited by succeeding waves of inmates. An analysis of patterns of laughter and anger, of sadness and irritability, of gait and gestures, has become a daily ritual among the political prisoners. I have been assured that, augmented by judicious and well-timed questions, it often yields very important news! And accurate! But I do not quite believe it at first, and my skepticism registers on my face.

One day, Gīcerū wa Njaū comes to my door, and he tells me, "I would like you to watch the faces of warders A, B, and C. Observe the fear in their eyes. See how they walk? Some major event to our advantage has occurred."

Throughout the day, I maintain a careful watch on the said faces. Alas, their faces yield nothing to me. But later in the week, news leaks out. The commissioner of prisons, Andrew Saikwa, has been dismissed, and Edward P. Lokopoyet, the SSP in charge of Kamītī, has been transferred to another prison.

I have never seen anything like it. The old SSP comes to introduce the new SSP (a Mr. James Mareka). When he announces his own imminent departure from Kamītī, the political prisoners actually clap in a collective spontaneous delirium of joy even before they know how the new SSP will turn out to be.

For me, relief too. The old SSP will never now demand to read and approve "my poems." I have never anyway written poetry, in or outside prison.

* * *

For a while, the reliefless senseless cruelty ends, and Kamĩtĩ under the new SSP becomes, relatively speaking, a paradise.

The new SSP ends the practice of locking up political prisoners for twenty-three hours a day. He will deal professionally and legally but reasonably with the occasional defiance of prison regulations and rules. He makes clear that he will not be a pushover. But there will be no more collective punishment unless there is a collective insurrection. Our cells will be opened at six in the morning and locked at five in the afternoon. We shall now be in our cells for thirteen instead of twenty-three hours.

The new SSP allows us to form our own committee for settling any disputes between us political prisoners, and as a vehicle through which we can present complaints that affect us all. Gĩcerũ and I will be on this committee throughout the rest of our stay. The other members, at different times, are Wasonga Sijeyo, Hadji Dagan, Mohamed Abdilie Hadow, and Ali Dubat.

The new SSP orders the reconnection of the radio, and for the first time, we can hear Voice of Kenya and foreign news, such as it is, and listen to sounds of music, such as it is. We dance to the sound of music. On the concrete corridor. The new SSP promises us a guitar!

The new SSP allows us to start classes. Most of the Somalis join English classes conducted by Mũhoro wa Mũthoga, popularly known as Fujika. Now he acquires another name—Mwalimu. His cell, no. 9, becomes a school.

The new SSP allows us to buy our own newspapers: the *Weekly Review*, *The Standard*, the *Daily Nation*, and *Taifa Leo*. They are ruthlessly censored wherever there's a reference to any one of us, but that's a small price to pay for the privilege of a little contact with the outside world. Better a newspaper with holes all over than no newspaper at all.

"During your reign," Wasonga Sijeyo tells the new SSP in a vote of thanks on behalf of us all, "we shall be free!"— meaning that his humaneness is a good omen.

* * *

That's how we come to learn about events like the Ogaden War between Ethiopia and Somalia and the uprising in Shaba (aka Katanga) Province against the Zairean regime of Joseph Mobutu, and the subsequent invasion and occupation of the area by the French to protect Euro-American investments.

That's how we come to learn about the heart surgeon Professor Christiaan Barnard's visit to Kenya as a guest of the attorney general, Charles Njonjo, and about his open defense of racism and apartheid, and his insulting advocacy of ties between Kenya and the dying regime of South Africa.

I incorporate his visit into my novel.

* * *

Writing it makes me better able to cope with life in the block, almost as if, through "stolen" pen and "stolen" toilet paper, I am in daily combat against the forces that had incarcerated me. Most important, time flies.

* * *

In the newspapers one day, I see Mĩcere Mũgo, pictured during the 1978 Kenya Schools Drama Festival at the British-run Kenya National Theatre, denouncing the continued dominance of foreign imperialist cultural interests in Kenya, and my heart leaps in joy.

Mīcere, a colleague in the literature department at the University of Nairobi, and I co-authored *The Trial of Dedan Kĩmathi* to rescue him from political and literary burial. Kĩmathi was still buried at Kamĩtĩ prison, but he will forever live in the collective memory of the Kenyan people. Like Waiyaki before him. Like Koitalel before him. Like Me Katilili and Otenyo and Nyanjirũ and many other heroes before him.

* * *

On another day, I read news of Charles Njonjo's launching of Yusuf Kodwavwala Dawood's novel *No Strings Attached* (Spear Books, Kenya, 1978) at a ceremony in the Serena Hotel. I read with interest his unstinted praise of the novel, its good, correct, grammatical English, and his attack on those who launch books without first reading them, books moreover that attack the government. I note that while reaffirming the right to freedom of expression, he warns Kenyan authors "not to write about things which might embarrass the government in the eyes of the public."

Dawood's novel is published by Heinemann, and the reported occasion takes me back to the launching of one of my novels, *Petals of Blood*, by Mwai Kibaki, then minister for finance, in July 1977 at the City Hall, Nairobi. *Petals of Blood* had also been published by Heinemann, which had hailed the book as a major publishing event! Kibaki had certainly read the novel. He made a speech in defense of literary and intellectual freedom that made him the talk of the university community for the next few months. His words now come back to me with the terrible force of historical irony:

> It is true that writers all over the world want to write and comment on what is going on in their own country of origin. But one of the most terrible things about the modern world is how many writers have had to emigrate to another nation in order to be able to comment on what's going on in their own country of origin. And it is a tragedy because it means that societies are themselves becoming intolerant, whereas the true freedom in any democratic system should be—as we are trying to do in this country; we have not succeeded yet, but we are trying that those who differ and those who take a different view of the society we live in must be able to paint what picture they see, so that we can have many, many pictures of the kind of Kenya we are living in now, because the efforts by some of the people in the media who write short quick stories, who try to present one picture only, is of course misleading. . . . At least let us give encouragement to those who spend their lifetime writing, commenting on the society that we live in. There is not very much else that we can do but at least we can give them that particular kind of recognition.

Exactly five months later I was in Kamĩtĩ Maximum Security Prison for helping to write a play in the Gĩkũyũ language, *Ngaahika Ndeenda*. Strange ways of encouraging Kenyan literature!

* * *

Fear of death suddenly dampens our happiness. Shikuku has been on a hunger strike for some days because the authorities have refused to allow him crutches to enable him to walk without crawling against the walls. Shikuku has been on other hunger strikes in prison whenever his rights to medical care and medical prescriptions have not been met. He fights for his rights and is admired for this by fellow political prisoners.

I had heard about hunger strikes before, but only in books and newspapers, never in real life. Every time Shikuku has been on a hunger strike, I thought he would die. In January, when most of the others were in Mombasa, he had come to my cell and had allowed me to read all his previous letters to the authorities related to his hunger strikes, just in case.

The police and the prison authorities would wait until he was on the verge of total collapse. Then they would come for him and rush him to hospital where he would be forcibly fed through the veins. Two or three days later, they would bring him back to prison.

But this time, it seems to us all, he is in a critical condition. They have kept him for four days. No food. No water. Fifth day. The same. "They want him to die," we whisper among ourselves. On the sixth day, he collapses. We are all locked up in our cells. They come for him with a stretcher.

We don't talk about it. But we are all sure that he is dead. A sense of impending doom grips the whole compound.

On the fifth day, he is brought back. Without the crutches. But with promises. A few days later, when it is clear that the crutches will not be forthcoming, Shikuku goes on yet another hunger strike.

They come for him on the fourth day of the strike. But this time they don't bring him back to cell 11. They take him to an isolation cell in G block to live alone, and we never see him again until the day of our release. But we know he is alive because he keeps on sending guards for books!

A hunger strike is premised on a readiness to die if one's demands are not met, and also on the assumption that the other party fears the moral or political consequences of one's death. But what a terrible thing to watch death knocking at the door of a Kenyan simply because he has made a principled stand on national issues.

* * *

In detention, when one is not reduced to the level of a beast, one is certainly treated like a child. You cannot be trusted with sharp weapons because you might take your own life. If you want to shave, you beg for a razor blade from the corporal in charge and then must promptly give it back.

In defiance, I start keeping a razor blade hidden in the cracks of my desk. I don't need it. It's simply a way of affirming my freedom and responsibility over my life!

* * *

An earth tremor. (I later learned that a minor earthquake shook the Eastern Highlands and Nairobi, measuring over 5 on the Richter scale!) Wish it were a social tremor to bring an end to the system and to this prison!

* * *

Games. Tenniquoit. Ludo. Chess. Checkers. Walks on the side-pavements.

* * *

We organize story-telling sessions. Ali Dubat and Wasonga Sijeyo are mines of folklore.

* * *

Singing, too! Religious hymns. Popular tunes. Political songs.

* * *

There is a guard who hardly ever talks. But when we start read-ing news of the exploits of the Red Brigades in Italy, his mouth suddenly opens. He can talk endlessly about them. With only one constant refrain. "And they are not touching the poor," he would say, laughing until tears flow down his cheeks. Then he would describe graphically, in minute detail, how they shot this or that rich Italian person, as if he had been present when the deed was done. "And to know that they are not touching the poor!" he would repeat. About Kenya or Africa, however, he is absolutely mum. No words. No opinions.

* * *

The new SSP releases old issues of *Time* and *Newsweek*. They are given to Kamĩtĩ Prison by the United States Information Service in Nairobi. For a week or so we revel in world events as seen through American eyes. But the pleasure of a newspaper or a news magazine is reading between the lines, if you know the publisher's or the writer's general view. There can be no totally objective newspaper—much less an American one.

I come across a *Newsweek* carrying an interview with Kofi Awoonor, the Ghanaian novelist and poet who had been incarcerated by the military dictator Ignatius Kutu Acheampong for a year without trial. I first met Kofi at Makerere, Kampala, during the historic 1962 Conference of African Writers of English Expression,[3] attended by, among others, Wole Soyinka, Chris Okigbo, Chinua Achebe, Langston Hughes, Saunders Redding, Ezekiel Mphahlele, Lewis Nkosi, Arthur Maimane, Bloke Modisane, Grace Ogot, Rebecca Njau, and Jonathan Kariara. I was then a student at Makerere just beginning to write: one or two published stories, two unpublished manuscripts, but with hope, great hope for an East African literary renaissance. What I remember most about the conference was the energy and the hope and the dreams and the confidence: after all, we were part of a continent emerging from a colonial era into . . . what? We never answered the question, but the hopes and dreams and the confidence remained. Now we have no doubt, two decades later, about the answer.

Now as I look at Kofi's picture in *Newsweek* at Kamītī Prison, I remember that Chris Okigbo, who led the conference with the paper "What Is African Literature?" is dead, a victim of an intrabourgeois war, which, in the words of Kole Omotoso, was merely for "redefining the land boundaries rather than redefining the quality of life for those who live within the existing boundaries," a war in which only the Americans, the British, and the French emerged as victors. I remember that Wole Soyinka and Kofi Awoonor have served prison terms for saying that things that aren't right *are not right*, and

I remember that many African writers have witnessed and recorded the terrible anguish of Africans killing innumerable Africans so that Euro-American capital can thrive on grounds made more fertile by African flesh and blood!

Bitter memories—but it's good just to see Awoonor's picture[4] and know that he is free and is continuing to denounce Africa's tin gods who jump at any little criticism of their corrupt regimes. This earth, our earth, my brother!

* * *

In another *Newsweek*, I come across a story about my detention without trial. The main story has been censored, but the censor had forgotten that the story ran on to a different column on a different page. *Newsweek* quotes "usually reliable" Nairobi intellectual circles as describing me as "a naive ideologue" for not knowing the limits of dissent and therefore not living within the restrictive walls of self-censorship.

I laugh at this! A naive ideologue? For writing in a Kenyan language? For joining hands with peasants to build a modern people-based Kenyan theater? For communicating with at least a few peasants? This is not dissent even. Not yet. Ideologue? And them, counter-ideologues. That's fair.

If sophistication means writing in a foreign language and taking a pro-imperialist, anti-Kenyan line in national and international affairs, then avaunt, sophistication! Quit my sight! If naïveté means writing about the heroism of Kenyan people in their centuries of struggle against any and every form of foreign economic, political, and cultural domination, then come, naïveté, let me embrace thee forever.

The Kenyan peasants were described as "naive" by their educated brethren when they challenged the might of the British empire, on whose shores the sun never set. Led by the Kenya Land and Freedom Army, the naive peasants took up arms against British imperialism in Kenya when their sophisticated brethren, fresh from seats of learning in Makerere, Harvard, Cambridge, London, Oxford, and elsewhere, were crying out (in sophisticated languages of course): hold it, we have been taught that imperialism is mighty and we should willingly become its slaves and get international prizes for being its faithful spokesmen.

Intellectual slavery masquerading as sophistication is the worst form of slavery.

Viva the "naive" peasants and workers of Kenya! Viva the glorious history of Kenyan people! I shout loudly in my heart, in my cell later.

* * *

I hear a siren from the other side. It's a mournful, terrible sound, like a mother bereaved of all her children. In this case, I'm told it's the prison alert for escaped prisoners.

I used to teach Dennis Brutus's book of poems, *Sirens Knuckles Boots*, but I never really understood the title. Now I do. I read his *Letters to Martha* more avidly. His opening letter captures very accurately the emotions of a new political prisoner:

>After the sentence
>mingled feelings:
>sick relief,
>the load of the approaching days

apprehension—
the hints of brutality
have a depth of personal meaning;

exultation—
the sense of challenge,
of confrontation,
vague heroism
mixed with self-pity
and tempered by the knowledge of those
who endure much more
and endure

* * *

Tuesday, June 13, 1978: Gĩcerũ corners me to give another lesson in body language. He tells me, "Now I would like you to watch the faces of the same warders, A, B, and C. See how they walk? See how they laugh? It is not good for us!"

It is early in the morning. And yes, they walk jauntily, they are laughing, and they are being a bit too jovial with political prisoners.

At three o'clock, we learn that the police have intervened. The radio is disconnected. And we can no longer buy or read newspapers.

When he is later confronted by political prisoners about this vindictiveness, the political prisoners' security officer, Mr. Mũhĩndĩ Mũnene, replies, "What would then be the meaning of detention?"

Ah, well: at least it's good to know that the ill treatment and torture in prison are not the result of personal aberration on the part of a few guards and officers, but that it is calculated and directed from the top.

But we shall never forget the relative humaneness of Mūhīndī Mūnene, the new SSP.

* * *

We go back to our games, to our books, to our pens, to our religions, to our story telling, to our monotonous lives, to our dreams of freedom.

* * *

Then Kenyatta died. And suddenly our dreams of freedom grew wings.

8

Dreams of Freedom

1

For those who wait in prison, as for those who wait outside, dreams of freedom start at the very minute of arrest. Something might just happen; maybe somebody will intervene; and even when everything seems against any possibility of release, there's the retreat to the final bravado: the plight can end only in either death or freedom, which I suppose are two different forms of release. So release of one sort or other is eventually assured.

But when? One of the cruelties of detention without trial and conviction—unlike ordinary imprisonment—is precisely this not knowing when one will get out. As for ordinary convicted prisoners—we are not talking of the fairness or unfairness of the trial, the so-called justice involved—they know the duration of their sentence, and no matter how long it is, their emotions and intellect can adjust to the fact and the reality. Not so the political detainee: they can be released after an hour, a day, a week, or after fifty years! So whether they like it or not, every minute, every hour of the day, the question lurks somewhere in their consciousness: Could it be now, today? Every guard's clinking of chains, every unexpected knock at the door, brings this question to the fore: Is it now, today? When? Some people ask, were you tortured in detention? But detention without trial is itself torture, and the greatest part of it is this ignorance of when. Yes, torture not only for those inside, but even for those outside the prison walls.

On September 19, 1978, Nyambura wrote me a letter in which she told me about the progress that Thiong'o, Kīmunya, Ngĩna, Ndũcũ, Mũkoma, and Wanjikũ were making in their different schools. Then she added:

"In your letter you told me that the state authorities have never asked you about your writings: what do they ask you when you go for questioning? I hear that all political prisoners are questioned or that their cases are reviewed every three or six months. How has your case been?"

She was asking about the Detainees Review Tribunal, so much trumpeted by the Kenya ruling authorities whenever questions of release of detained persons were raised in world councils. The eight-member Detainees Review Tribunal chaired by Justice Alan R.W. Hancox (a British ex-judge of the Kenyan High Court) met every six months, and served three political purposes: as a public relations team to allay national and international fears regarding the government's prison conditions; as a screening team, just like those of the Emergency era in colonial Kenya; and finally but basically, as an instrument of torture, part of the state's psychological terror wielded against the individual political prisoner and the nation as a whole.

As a hoax to national and world opinion, the tribunal was

excellent: its very existence and its six-monthly motions of pretense at review—expenses and the trip to Mombasa fully paid—gave the intended impression that those not released had somehow not satisfied this very impartial tribunal. And to many, the fact that the Detainees Review Tribunal was chaired by a foreigner was the final evidence of its impartiality. Its carefully nursed impression of impartiality, its quasi-judicial character (in theory a political prisoner could have the services of a lawyer)—tended to establish a prima facie case against the poor political prisoner. Either the prisoner had refused to cooperate or the tribunal, after carefully weighing the evidence, had, in its judicial wisdom, found the petitioner still unfit for "human" company. The political prisoner was tried (for unknown crimes of course) and found wanting.

The fact was that in its entire membership, the eight-man Review Tribunal was a wholly civil service affair. And the fact that it was chaired by a foreigner, far from inclining it to impartiality, would the more likely have inclined it to partiality toward the state of which the tribunal was a part. In my case, my unstated reasons for detention were my consistent opposition to the foreign control of our economy and culture, and to the mental colonialism in the ruling comprador bourgeoisie, which gives them a childlike faith in foreigners per se, especially if such foreigners happen to be British or American. The foreign chairmanship of the tribunal was to me one more proof of my correct position. Could one then expect colonial foreigners to make judgments against themselves?

By the very nature of their position, foreigners tend to feel that it is not for them to make controversial pronouncements on the basic questions of democratic and human rights in the country of their temporary but well-paid adoption. "We gave them independence; let them make a mess of it if that's what they want," tends to be the general attitude of those from an imperialist country working as "experts" in a former colony. Yet they are thoroughly enjoying the fruits of that mess. Why care? Who cares?

Such a foreigner might even pretend not to feel or not to see the mess. At any rate, there is no way such a foreigner can feel loyalty to the Kenyan history of struggle or feel the pressures for democracy that loyalty demands. There is a chance that Kenyans, depending on their class sympathies, might feel these pressures and loyalty, and perchance their sense of duty to the nation might compel them to arrive at a position similar to the one held by the Indian Supreme Court: "Preventive detention is a serious invasion of personal liberty and such meagre safeguards as the constitution has provided against the improper exercise of the power must be jealously watched and enforced by the courts."

In our case, there was no hope of such a pronouncement. For even assuming that the tribunal was impartial, it had only advisory powers; its advice to the government was never made public, and it was never communicated to political prisoners.

It was in its proceedings, however, that the tribunal's role as a screening team came through. As far as I know, no political prisoner was ever told of the government's charges against them. The tribunal sat there and simply asked the political prisoners to tell them whatever it was that they wanted communicated to the government. It was a most weird experience. Not only were the prisoners prejudged to be guilty, but the burden of self-prosecution fell on them. In other words, one was to be one's own accuser, prosecutor, and witness against oneself.

But even after going through all that, one could never be sure of release. The prisoners had to prove themselves guilty beyond any and every reasonable doubt and to crown this confession with abject pleas for presidential mercy and clemency. Even then, they were not sure of release, and after six months the tribunal would come for more proofs of one's assumed guilt and more pleas for mercy, without deigning to say what had been the reception of the previous self-prosecution and abject pleas. The Detainees Review Tribunal, then, clearly saw its role as one of receiving a political prisoner's list of confessions and pleas and carrying them to the government for a thorough scrutiny by the Special Branch.

Its being an instrument of mental torture consisted in its raising of false hopes. Twice a year, the Detainees Review Tribunal would meet, raise people's hopes, and then dash them to the ground. Even when a political prisoner intellectually convinced themselves—after four or six or twenty appearances—that the tribunal was at best an ineffectual body for a government cover-up and at worst a screening team, they still retained a faint hope that maybe this time . . . After three or five years, a number of political prisoners had resolved not to see the tribunal again and had written to say so.

I appeared before the tribunal twice. The first appearance, after fourteen days at Kamĩtĩ, was in the SSP's offices. Incredible as it might seem, despite what the other political prisoners had told me about it, I still went there with some hope: since what I had done had been completely aboveboard in a democratic society, maybe someone might have thought it over and decided on the futility of detaining truth. Once the tribunal told me about the charges against me, I would be able to convince them of my innocence.

The first tribunal, at Kamĩtĩ—I and a few others were not flown to Mombasa as was the usual practice—was chaired by Acting Justice Abdul Majid Cockar in the absence of Justice Alan Hancox, who was then reportedly on leave in Britain. After polite introductions, they simply stared at me. I asked them why I was detained. They didn't know. What were the accusations against me? They didn't know. But now the chairman spoke. Had I anything I wanted to tell the government?

The second tribunal, also at Kamĩtĩ, was held in July, and this time it was chaired by Justice Hancox. This time I had written a memorandum, putting in writing my verbal complaints to the first tribunal and expanding on them. I wanted to state my position vis-à-vis issues of language, literature, culture, and foreign domination very clearly and very finally. In my memorandum, it was the government that was on trial. My detention without trial for advocating a national culture, free from imperialist domination, was major evidence against the regime. Again the same silent stares. And the same question: What more, apart from what was in the memorandum, did I want to tell the government?

The only difference between the first session in January and the second in July was in the chairmanship. Justice Cockar had been a bit more patient; he was at least willing, or seemed willing, to listen. He noted down anything that I wanted to say. Then the whole interview lasted slightly more than five minutes. Justice Hancox was impatient, yawned several times and kept looking at his watch. This time the interview lasted less than three minutes.

I always looked at the faces of other political prisoners, and I could see the anxieties occasioned by the nearness of the tribunal. Dreams of freedom were eating into their peace of mind. I myself found it difficult to sleep on the eve of the two sessions. But after the interview, an incredible hollowness would seize me. It took more than two weeks to compose myself into waiting for the next session. I was determined, though, that the second appearance would, for me, be the last. I would thereafter join those who had said that they would not be a party to the gigantic judicial hoax. It was far better to nurse one's dreams of freedom in privacy and know that they were only dreams and wishes, rather than have them used against you, like Tantalus of old: you were shown the way to quench your thirst for freedom, but on arrival at the gate the way was but an iron barrier and the Detainees Review Tribunal merely watchmen at the gate.

Wasonga Sijeyo once called me aside and told me never to build any certainty of release on false hopes: "It is good to have faith, to keep on hoping. For what is life, but hope? Never prevent a man from hoping, for if you do, you are denying him reasons for living. To hope for a better tomorrow, to dream of a new world, that is what is human. But don't be so certain of the hour and the day as to let it break you if the hoped-for freedom does not come at the expected hour and day."

We sat on the pavement facing the stone walls that divided our compound from that of the Kenyans condemned to die.

Then he told me about his past experiences with dreams of freedom. On at least three occasions, he had been very sure of release. The first dream had its origins in a strong rumor from the guards at Kamĩtĩ and was given substance by certain assurances from the tribunal at its sitting in Shimo La Tewa Prison, Mombasa. He waited, unable to sleep, hope climbing on hope. Nothing came of it. The second had even greater substance. It was after a Luo delegation had visited Kenyatta. The delegation was promised Wasonga's release. A prison officer even told him to be ready, for he could be summoned to Kenyatta's presence any day, any hour. For a week or so, he lay awake, riding on tenterhooks of hope. Nothing came of this.

The third dream that seemed almost a reality was the furthest from reality, a nightmare, really, and it was clearly meant to destroy him forever. Again he was told to get ready. He packed his luggage, all the precious little things that one accumulates in prison, and got into his civilian clothes. But at the gate, the officers looked at the official documents and announced in hurt surprise the late discovery of an elementary error that even a child could have detected. "Very sorry, Mr. Sijeyo, but it was not you."

Because of these experiences, Wasonga was the most reserved and cautious whenever there were any individual or collective jubilations at rumors of imminent release.

2

One such premature jubilation was based on revelations from the Koran; what later came to be known as the Koran theory of freedom. Islam was introduced into the compound by members of the Kenya Somali nationality.

Ahmed Shurie and Mohamed Abdilie led the daily festi-

val of five prayer sessions (facing Mecca) and a feast of songs
in Arabic and Somali. Before the arrival of the Somalis, the
only religion was Christianity in the form of two of its major
divisions—Catholic and Protestant, led by Father Lawless and
Reverend Ngarī. Now the two largest world religions, Islam
and Christianity, and their two rival books of God, the Koran
and the Bible, contended for adherents at Kamītī Prison.

The Military Man and I were the only political prisoners
who belonged to neither camp. Instead we would play a game
of chess or else stand by and watch the proceedings from afar.
Islam was the first and only one to make a dramatic conquest.
Adam Mathenge, previously a Catholic, became a Muslim.
The ceremony of conversion took place on Monday, January 30, at 1:30 p.m. and was watched by all the political prisoners. He became Adam Ahamed and he wore a Muslim cap. I
didn't see any Muslim become a Christian.

I was fascinated by the two religions, especially by the differences between them. The Muslims at Kamītī believed in
the literal truth of every word in the Koran, with no room
for interpretation or metaphor. They told me that the Koran
was not just a book. Like the Torah of Judaism, it contained
a way of life, a culture that regulated all of a person's actions.
Because it looked more reduced to ritual, Islam seemed the
more demanding of the two religions: five prayer sessions a day
and, for those aspiring to religious leadership, recital of the
whole Koran from the first to the last page, once a week. For
Islam's adherents, the Koran was a world. The Christian Bible,
on the other hand, did not contain a rigid way of life, a totality
of culture or rules governing daily behavior, and for its adherents, especially at Kamītī, it was not a world. Christianity was

certainly much less demanding in observance of ritual: there were group meetings only when the Protestant chaplain came to visit.

The Christian chaplain had told me, the Bible is a whole library. Sixty-six books. "You don't need any more." The Muslim sheikh used to tell me, "The Koran is the only book you need. It contains all the knowledge there has been, there is, and there will be." Both claimed that their book was the book of God. But it was the Muslims who seemed to believe more in their book as the infallible word of God, a word-for-word transcript of a tablet in heaven, as revealed to the Prophet Mohamed by the angel Gabriel, for they turned to it, read it, to find out what would happen tomorrow; for instance, who among the Muslim political prisoners would get a family visit and when.

Now Sheikh Ahmed Shurie read the Koran, and he saw the stars scattering away and oceans rolling, and it was revealed to him that we would all be released on Madaraka (Internal Self-Rule) Day by the grace of Jomo Kenyatta, though the order would come from God.

Thus June 1, 1978, saw a high temperature of expectation, especially among the Muslims. Most of the non-Muslims expressed doubts about the veracity of the revelations, but we all hoped that the prophecy would come true—whether through revelation or coincidence, it didn't matter. The calm dignity with which the sheikh kept on asserting the inevitability of our release and the way he would smile confidence at the doubters, made some of us suspect that maybe some friendly guard had whispered vital information to him. But a systematic, though not open, inquiry among the other Muslims revealed that the entire revelation came through the Koran, which was a more reliable source of truth and prophecy. One Muslim political prisoner had even packed his luggage, ready to bolt to freedom at any hour of the day or night.

Nothing of our freedom came on Madaraka Day. But so sure was he of the truth of the revelation that even on June 2—the newspapers had not yet been stopped—the sheikh asked that all the papers should be read carefully for any clue or hint about our impending release.

It turned out that Kenyatta's speech at Madaraka was the shortest ever, and it contained not a single word about the fate of political prisoners. But reading between the lines, we were all sure that Kenyatta was seriously ill.

3

It was about the same time that two doves started flying low over the compound, sometimes even perching and cooing on the high walls. Now emerged the dove theory of freedom. In Biblical Jewish mythology, the dove was the bird that brought the good news to Noah's Ark that all was now well with the earth and he could return home to land from his exile in the sea.

In some African mythology, the dove also plays an important role as the messenger of peace and hope. There is a beautiful Gĩkũyũ story in which dove, after being fed with castor-oil seeds by a pregnant woman whose life and that of her baby are threatened by a man-eating ogre, Irimũ, agrees to undertake a journey to go to her husband, a blacksmith, Mũturi, in his smithy, far away. It sings to him:

Smith smithing away
Cangarara—ĩca!
Smith smith quickly
Cangarara—ĩca!
Your wife has given birth
Cangarara—ĩca!
With a man-eater for a midwife
Cangarara—ĩca!

The dove sings so persistently and movingly that the smith at once goes back home and releases his wife from misery by killing the man-eater.

There is another story in which the dove puts together the bones of a dead girl and molds back her flesh using mud, then breathes life into her, and she walks back to her joyous parents with her former beauty multiplied tenfold.

Now, at Kamĩtĩ it turned out that the last three releases—of Achieng Oneko, John David Kali, and Samson Nthiwa—were each preceded by the mysterious sudden appearance of two doves, one of them actually landing in the yard. One political prisoner believed that if one of these current doves landed in the yard, it would be a sure sign of the imminent release, if not of all of us, of at least one, most likely himself—but a release all the same.

No doves landed in the prison yard. (When I arrived home after my release, I found doves in the yard. They had nested on the roof of the house. I asked Nyambura, "When did these birds come here?" She replied, "In January 1978, soon after your detention.") But the doves went on increasing in numbers, so that by December about twenty doves were making regular flights over the compound, eliciting many jokes about the dove theory of freedom, but also exciting fantasies of their flight in freedom. The dove theory of freedom and the heated controversy, fantasy, and speculation it aroused—much more than had been aroused by the Koran theory—recalled poem seventeen in Dennis Brutus's book, *Letters to Martha*:

> In prison
> the clouds assume importance
> and the birds
>
> With a small space of sky
> cut off by walls
> of bleak hostility
> and pressed upon by hostile authority
> the mind turns upwards
> . . .
>
> the complex aeronautics
> of the birds
> and their exuberant acrobatics
> become matters for intrigued speculation and won-
>   derment

Dennis Brutus, writing about his experiences in a South African prison in 1965, could now speak with uncanny insight to us at Kamītī, Kenya, in 1978, penned in a similar inglorious spot. Perhaps it is poem eleven from *Letters to Martha* that best sums up our experience with these successive dreams of freedom:

> Events have a fresh dimension,
> for all things can affect the pace
> of political development—
>
> but our concern
> is how they hasten or delay
> a special freedom—
> that of those the prisons hold
> and who depend on change
> to give them liberty.
>
> And so one comes to a callousness,
> a savage ruthlessness—
> voices shouting in the heart
> "Destroy! Destroy!"
> or
> "Let them die in Thousands!"—
> really it is impatience.

The last line is false as an explanation, though true as a description. The essence lies in the second stanza. For Robben Island in South Africa, as for Kamĩtĩ in Kenya, the poem speaks of a situation in which the release of political prisoners depends on the whims of a bourgeois dictatorship. For these prisoners, their final dream of freedom comes to rest on objective change to give them liberty.

4

When I first arrived in Kamĩtĩ, the one question that nearly all the groups shot at me was about Kenyatta's health. Quite innocently, I would tell them that Kenyatta was in excellent health. On hearing this, the group would drift away in silence without asking another question. It was Thairũ wa Mũthĩga who was to tell me the reason later: "Believe me but we have lost any hope of release through the tribunal or through presidential mercy. Since J.M. Kariũki's murder, no political prisoner has been released . . . sorry, there was Ochieng Oneko, but we believe he was released to mollify public opinion after the detention of Shikuku and Seroney. So our hope rests on Kenyatta's death. You don't believe me? No political prisoner is going to be released until after Kenyatta's death. That's our opinion, anyway. So when you told us that Kenyatta's health was excellent, you were crushing our hopes without your knowing it."

This theory of freedom—Kenyatta's death as the liberator—gained momentum, especially after the collapse of the Koran Madaraka theory and the refusal of the tribunals of January and July to release anybody, especially those like Mwanzia (in Shimo La Tewa), Ongongi Were, and Wasonga Sijeyo, going into their seventh, eighth, and tenth years respectively.

On Tuesday, August 22, we were locked in our cells at the usual time of 4:45 p.m. As was my daily habit, except when stuck in a writer's block, I now sat at the desk exorcising out of me all the images reflected in my mind during the day as I walked for exercise, or played tenniquoit or chess, or listened to arguments or narrations or reminiscences. The novel had become my most important weapon in the daily combat with the stony dragon.

A guard brought me a note from Wasonga Sijeyo: "The greatest has fallen or he is about to fall. Keep this to yourself. Will confirm tomorrow."

He had been reading Ali's autobiography, *The Greatest,* and I assumed that he was talking about the fall of Muhammad Ali from the boxing throne. But why the uncertainty? He had either fallen, in which case it was news, or he had not, in which case it was speculation, and speculation was no news. And why the caution: "Keep this to yourself? I wrote back another note, for my suspicions and curiosity were now aroused, and I could not wait until morning. "Do you mean THE greatest in boxing?" The reply came through the wall. Just one word, "No," and I there and then knew what was already public knowledge in Kenya, in the whole world, but for us political prisoners forbidden knowledge:

Jomo Kenyatta was dead.

In the morning I cornered Wasonga. He confirmed it: Kenyatta had died in his sleep while on a "busy working holiday in Mombasa." His last companions were a group of foreign emissaries. "But let's keep this to ourselves, for the time being. I myself will tell Koigi."

It was a rule among us political prisoners that the sources of one's information were always to be protected. We didn't want to jeopardize the job of any of our informants or cut off such sources of information.

It was a most terrible burden trying to keep this vital information from our fellow political prisoners—for it meant so much for each one of them—but we could not turn off the tap of information by committing any indiscretion. For a day, the three of us who carried the burden of our knowledge would speak a thousand silent questions with our eyes or faces, but none had the answer.

Gradually the news was passed to each political prisoner individually under the strictest promise not to show any feelings on his face, in his voice, or in his behavior toward officers and guards.

And so for three days, a game of hypocritical silence was played in Kamĩtĩ: the guards pretending that all was as usual and we pretending that we didn't understand their sudden absent-mindedness, their quick little surreptitious groupings, or their forced laughter. Now simple questions like "How is the weather outside?" or "How is life outside?" though spoken innocently, would suddenly acquire a special symbolism, and you'd see a warder cast a quick suspicious glance or else wince before recovering and trying to laugh off the inquiry.

It was a most unreal situation. There was an important drama in Kenya's history being played outside the walls, but here at Kamĩtĩ we were all pretense, actors in a theater of extreme absurdity.

Ironically, it was Reverend Ngarĩ, the Protestant chaplain, who broke down the walls of this dance of absurdity. For some reason, the chaplain had grown more likable over the year; those who had known him in previously said that they'd noticed a change of attitude toward political prisoners. He had grown less ready to preach at them as if he assumed their guilt and the government's benign benevolence. He had stopped talking as if all they needed to do was accept Jesus Christ as their personal Lord and Savior, confess all their past political sins, and go back to Kenyatta's paradise, the envy of the rest of godless Africa. Some of the political prisoners even started missing him; they'd ask, "When is Reverend Ngarĩ coming?" Or grow wistful: "Reverend Ngarĩ has deserted our compound these last few weeks."

Between him and me there had grown a mutual acceptance of each other's position. After our initial encounter, he never again tried to force his religion on me, and I in turn never questioned his right to believe in it. He would come, greet me, ask after my health or comment on the game of chess, and go to his religious sessions with the others. He had, though, some kind of victory over me.

One day he came with tapes containing a sermon by Reverend Gatū and challenged me, on the basis of my stated premises, to hear it: had I not in January asked him about sermons by Kenyan nationals? I attended the session, the only one I ever did, and heard Reverend Gatū at his oratorical best: he was attacking the leprosy of private property and property accumulation, basing his sermon on the text of the story of Ahab, who had stolen Naboth's vineyard, after Jezebel, Ahab's wife, had the poor man murdered. I could hardly believe my ears!

When on Friday, August 25, Reverend Ngarĩ came into the yard, he seemed disturbed. He didn't make the rounds greeting people; he certainly did not greet me, and twice he came in and out within a space of fifteen minutes before settling down to the usual religious session. But it turned out not to be the usual religious session. It was as if he sensed that the political prisoners had silently laid a trap for him: they wanted to see if he too—a proclaimed man of God—would participate in the grand deception. It was probably difficult for him, walking on the tightrope between his vows to his Christian conscience and his vows to his prison conscience. He resolved the conflict in prayer. In the course of the prayer and without mentioning names, he prayed to God to keep in peace the soul of the leader who had departed from among us and to guide the hand and heart of the one who had taken over the reins of power. Then he walked out of the compound to avoid responding to any direct questions!

Now the Muslims (and we, the two nonbelievers) surrounded the Christians to make them describe to us every word of the chaplain, every change of nuance and tone of his voice, every word of his sermon, his gestures and behavior, everything. It was as if the Koranic revelation had been or was about to be fulfilled through a sermon from the Christian Bible.

Even after this, the theater of absurdity went on, but now all the actors were police, prison officials, and guards. We were still officially ignorant of Kenyatta's death, and Daniel Arap Moi's takeover.

At one time, the guards were summoned by prison officials and put under the strictest orders with threats of dismissal not to reveal anything about Kenyatta's death to us or to reveal by word or gesture what was going on outside the walls.

So a game of deadly wit started: now that we knew about Kenyatta's death through a prayer, we could talk about it openly, and we no longer hid our feelings. Political prisoners would inquire as to whom they should now send their letters of supplication, and they would be told to write to Kenyatta. What address? State House, Nairobi, of course. So the joke started: "I am writing to Kenyatta, the ex-political prisoner, c/o State House, Nairobi." But the officials were really to blame for these trite jokes, because they grimly held on to "their fact" that Kenyatta was not yet dead. How completely did they want a man to die in order to say he was dead?

When Ali Dubat, who had gone for an operation, was finally discharged from the hospital, he was not returned to the compound, but to an isolation cell in G block. His fault? The natural possession of two ears. While he was in the hospital, a hysterical nurse had rushed in shouting the news of Kenyatta's death. He remained in that punishment cell until the day of his release three months later.

5

It is difficult to describe the feelings occasioned in me by Kenyatta's death. I had met him only once, in 1964 at Gatũndũ. I was then working as a reporter with the *Daily Nation*. The occasion was May Day 1964, and a group of peasants from Mũrang'a had come to donate relief money for their class counterparts in Nyanza, victims of floods on the Kano Plains. Oginga Odinga was present, a witness of this act of class solidarity. For some reason, I and the *Nation* photographer were the only journalists present. I still retain a photograph of Kenyatta, Odinga, and me taken at the time. I am standing, with a notebook and pen in hand, probably putting a question to the big two, the peasants crowding around us. It was a brief, a very brief, first and last encounter.

However, in my novels—*Weep not, Child*; *A Grain of Wheat*; and *Petals of Blood*—Kenyatta has either appeared directly as a historical figure or has been hinted at in the portrayal of some of the characters. In 1964 a publisher asked me to write Kenyatta's biography, and for a time I played with the idea before rejecting it. I was not sure if I could get official permission and the family cooperation necessary for such a task. I also felt—which was true—that I was then too young, too inexperienced, and too confused in social outlook to cope with the literary and political demands of putting together a definitive biography. The idea resurfaced briefly in 1968 when Ali Mazrui and I were traveling in the same plane from an international conference of Africanists in Dakar, Senegal, and we decided to attempt a joint biography. Mazrui wrote to Kenyatta, c/o President's Offices, Nairobi, to seek permission for that undertaking. He did not get it.

In a way, it was good that we didn't get permission. Our outlooks would have clashed in the interpretation. Mazrui's analysis of the African situation starts with tribe; mine, with class.

Even without a clash of outlook, I'm not sure if we could have done a finer job than Murray-Brown's *Kenyatta*. It is a revealing biography, less for his interpretation than for the impressive material he has unearthed and brought together between hard covers. Murray-Brown could not get at the Kenyatta brought to dramatic life by the very material he himself had assembled.

There were then several Kenyattas, but they can be reduced to four. There was the Kenyatta of the era of the Kikuyu Central Association (KCA), who made anti-imperialist statements and declarations valid for that time. He was then truly a spokesman of the peasants and workers, and he took up the cause of the peasants of the various nationalities in Kenya: Wakamba, Abaluhya, Dholuo, Gĩkũyũ, Giriama, Maasai, the lot. He articulated the need and necessity for a revolutionary unity of peasants and workers of Kenya to overthrow British imperialism.

There was the Kenyatta of the era of the Kenya African Union (KAU). This Kenyatta was a graduate of Malinowski's school of anthropology at London University, a cultural nationalist (he had written *Facing Mount Kenya*, in which politics was deliberately cut out), who for fifteen years had quite literally been out of physical touch with the living struggles of the Kenyan people. KAU was a nationalist organization grouping a variety of classes under its constitutional nonviolence umbrella. It had no quarrel with capitalism, only with the exclusion of Africans, on the basis of race, from full participation in it.

Then there was the Kenyatta of the era of the Kenya African National Union (KANU): a prison graduate, an ex–political prisoner who for nine years had again been out of physical touch with the living struggle as led by Kenya Land and Freedom Army (KLFA, Mau Mau). The liberation army had been weakened politically and militarily, especially after the capture and execution of the leader, Dedan Kĩmathi, and hence it was not in a position to force adoption of certain programs by KANU.

And then there was the Kenyatta of KANU in power, who made sure that anybody associated with the militant nationalism of the KLFA were never anywhere near the seats of power.

Because of his composite history, in looking at Kenyatta, all the classes could see a bit of themselves in him and tended to see what they wanted to see rather than what there was to see: petit bourgeois vacillations and opportunism.[1]

My reception of his death was then one of sadness. Even though he had wrongly jailed me, his death was not an occasion for rejoicing but one that called for a serious reevaluation of our history—so as to see the balance of losses and gains and work out the options open to us for the future of our children and country.

6

With Kenyatta's death, another dream of freedom possessed us all, and this time even Wasonga seemed to believe in the possibility. "We shall not be here for more than three years from now," he would tell us. Three years: not a particularly cheerful thought, but shorter than the ten years he had spent in the compound. Then suddenly a rumor started: we would be freed on Friday, September 22.

The whole compound was gripped with feverish excitement and expectations. A week to go, and we would all be free to talk with our families, see green life again, hear the sweet laughter of women and children! Food became completely tasteless, and on Tuesday evening very few touched their prison food. We exchanged addresses and confidences, and promises of future meetings. We started talking of detention and political imprisonment and Kamĩtĩ as things of history. Some of the prisoners had already arranged for new tire sandals, which they would carry home as a remembrance of things past.

The morning of Friday, September 22, found us still in the grip of hope. There had been no official word, but the rumor had become a reality. Why not? Every reasonable argument pointed to our release on that day. Some political prisoners had sat down, made a list of all cabinet members, and tried to determine their voting pattern in terms of yes or no to our release on that day, and naturally the ministers in favor of our release outnumbered those against us. A political prisoner who cautioned realism in our expectations was shouted down and denounced as an enemy of the people.

It was a kind of collective madness, I remember, and when at about ten o'clock there was a vigorous banging on the outer door and a prison officer dashed in waving his staff of office, I said to myself, *At long last, God—freedom!*

But others read something different. Quickly Koigi pulled me aside and whispered, "Go and clean your room at once! There is going to be a search!" and he literally ran toward his own cell to do the same.

I had never seen a prison search before and though the other political prisoners told me that under Edward Lokopoyet it had been a weekly ritual, I never really knew what it meant. So I was not sure what I was expected to do or how to prepare for it.

And then the warders descended upon us, from all sides, batons raised, literally hounding us back to our cells. There was no laughter in their eyes. My cell was the first to be raided.

9

Sherlock Holmes and the Strange Case of the Missing Novel

1

I didn't know what they were looking for, exactly. Razor blades, nails, weapons of violence? Letters, diaries, secret communications with the outside world? I had no contraband items, maybe the razor blade, but I could not think of anything else, and even if I could, where and how would I hide them, in front of their eyes?

Suddenly the sergeant saw scattered piles of toilet paper on the desk and pounced on them. Then, as if delirious with joy and triumph, he turned to the presiding officer and announced:

"Here is the book, sir, on toilet paper."

It dawned on me in that second that this was what they were after, and I felt paralyzed.

"Seize it!" the officer told him, "the whole lot! Who told you to write books in prison?" he continued, turning to me.

Soon every sheet of toilet paper on the desk had been put in a bag. They looked at one another satisfied at the loot.

But I was laughing inside, literally congratulating myself. In writing the novel, I had used several subterfuges to mislead the ever watchful guards as to what I was doing. First I had asked for pen and paper to write my "confession" to the Detainees Review Tribunal. I got pen all right, which was what I really wanted, but unfortunately, for writing material, they gave me a few sheets only. But wait! There was the toilet paper!

The toilet paper was square single sheets stacked to make a bundle between two slightly harder covers, top and bottom, held together by a tape. In appearance each bundle looked like a notebook without a spine. The paper itself was not the soothing, softy-softie kind. It was actually hard, meant to punish prisoners, but it turned out be great writing material, really holding up to the ballpoint pen very well. What was hard for the body was hardy for writing on.

I created a not too elaborate visual make-belief that I was writing my confession. In reality, I was drafting a novel on the toilet paper. But how was I to hide the written material? I thought it best to hide it in the open but use a kind of decoy to take their eyes away from the finished drafts. It was simple. I left all the discarded drafts on the desk, quite a pile. But for the finished draft I put it back into the notebook-like bundle, but in the middle, leaving the top and the bottom layer with clean sheets. Then I would put the original tape back. Looking at it from the side, it looked like a clean unused bundle of toilet paper.

I had to use my share of toilet bundles, with the other fellow prisoners giving what of theirs they could spare. The problem was that the pile of the novel toilet paper at the corner of the room was becoming higher and higher.

So it was with a sense of triumph that I saw them collect the discarded drafts on the table and put them in a bag. They were about to leave my room when one of the guards stopped by the pillar of toilet paper at the corner. "You are allowed only two bundles at any one time," he shouted, and the officer motioned him to seize them as well. They had to bring in another basket, but I was no longer looking at what they were doing. All I could sense with the pain of a thousand knife stabs was that they had put all the bundles in a basket and left the cell.

It was as if I had been drained of all life. My novel, written with blood, sweat, and toil on toilet paper had been seized! Only two chapters hidden in between the empty back pages of a Bible Koigi had lent me remained. The Bible lay there on the desk as if mocking me, "If you had trusted all the Warīnga novel to me, you would have saved it all."

Gloom fell over Kamītī. Every political prisoner had lost something. We had been deliberately lulled into slumber by the carefully circulated rumor of release. But most political prisoners had developed fantastic cunning, which had made them act like lightening, and many had saved a lot of their prison notes. I had suffered the major loss and the other political prisoners clearly felt with me. I was grateful for the group solidarity. But it didn't lessen the hurt.

Only a writer can possibly understand the pain of losing a manuscript, any manuscript. With this novel I had struggled with language, with images, with prison, with bitter memories, with moments of despair, with all the mentally and emotionally adverse circumstances in which one is forced to operate while in custody, and now it had gone.

The next three weeks were the worst of my stay at Kamītī.

Nevertheless I made a new resolution: no matter what happened, I would start all over again. I would reconstruct the novel in between the printed lines of a Chekhov, or a Gorky, or a Mann, or of the Bible—I would even ask the chaplain for three or four Bibles of different sizes as evidence of a new-found devotion! It would not be the same novel, but I would not accept defeat.

I never had the occasion to try out my resolution, though I did scribble the plot and the few sequences of events I could recollect in a volume of Chekhov's short stories—*The Lady with a Lap Dog*. After about three weeks, on October 18, the new SSP returned the Warĩnga manuscript to me.

"I see nothing wrong with it," he said. "You write in very difficult Kikuyu!" he added.

"Thank you!" was all I said, but he will probably never know the depth of the emotion behind those two words.

"But you should never have written it on toilet paper," he went on. "I'll ask the chief warder to supply you with scrap paper—there is plenty of it in my office—so you can transfer the whole thing from toilet paper."

I shut myself in my room for a reunion with my novel.

Write on, brother.
Write on!
My star still reigns!

I look into the bag, puzzled. Something is not right. Then I realize all too suddenly that what they have returned is the discarded drafts that they had collected from the table! My cleverness has caught up with me. Was this an elaborate joke, a hoax, on the part of the prison authorities? Return to me only that portion that I had pretended to be the novel?

2

I turn to the chief warder, the one in charge of the block. He says they have given me back everything they got back from SSP. I say no, they still have the biggest portion of the book. He takes my complaint back to the SSP. The SSP comes to the compound in person and reassures me that he returned everything, but he promises to check and recheck his own office and home. I detect no malice in his gait or look or tone of voice. The report the following day is the same. What he gave back was all he had.

A mystery. Between my cell and the SSP office, my novel has disappeared without trace. It becomes the case of the missing novel on toilet paper. Everybody starts playing Sherlock Holmes. After a day or two, turning over and over the same speculation, they give up, puzzled, but with some content in simply asserting that they knew that the guards really knew what had happened to the novel.

Gĩcerũ, the same reader of body languages, does not give up, even after nearly all of us have suspended our amateur detective work. He notices, according to him afterward, that now and then, as the guards in our block leave for home, they would each help themselves to a bundle of fresh toilet paper. He observed the pattern for about a week. One day, he deliberately strays into the warders' office in our block to ask for something totally irrelevant, but as the Chief warder turns around to look for the something, Gĩcerũ quickly peers at a basket in the corner. It was full of bundles of toilet paper.

He worked out what had happened. When the warders raided my room and seized my bundles of toilet paper, they put them into the basket. Then as they went to the other rooms and seized their unused bundles, they simply put them on top of my bundles of my novel.

Gĩcerũ comes back to me and reports: your novel must be in the basket, and since the SSP has given the okay for its return, ask to see what's in the basket. Which I did. The warder shrugs his shoulders, as if he has nothing to hide, and points to the basket. The surprise on his face told me that even he did not know anything about what I now saw:

My entire novel, in jumbled bundles of toilet paper, was in the basket. It never left the block. They had assumed that the pile of bundles they had seized from my room had indeed been unused pile of toilet paper. And their only concern was that I was hoarding toilet paper when every cell was allowed only two bundles at any on time. Gĩcerũ, our Sherlock Holmes, solved the mystery in the nick of time. All the unused bundles had been taken. The very next one would have been a chapter or several chapters of the novel I had written on toilet paper.

10

Devil on the Cross

Waringa ngatha ya wira. . . . Waringa heroine of toil there she walks haughtily carrying her freedom in her hands. . . .

No!

There she walks knowing that . . . There she walks carrying . . . knowing . . .

No!

She walked outside knowing that greater struggles . . .

I try different combinations. Now and then I look at the walls for a word, a name, a sentence. The walls of cell 16 have become my dictionary of words and music.

Since the big fiasco of September 22, dreams of freedom have given way to nightmares of a longer stay in this dungeon. Other dates on which freedom was expected, like Kenyatta Day, though not with the same intensity of September 22, have proved to be receding mirages. The Koran no longer yields its secrets. The man of the Bible has not been seen. The doves keep on flying in increasing numbers, but none lands on the grounds.

People are silent about predictions. I no longer mention

my invitation to a roast goat party at my home on December 25. Life has come to an ominous standstill. No more games of chess, Ludo, checkers, tenniquoit. Walks on the side-pavements have become more popular. But now the main talk is about the necessity to brace ourselves for the nightmare of a longer stay in prison.

Although I, too, have been affected by the new mood of pessimism, every night I have kept faith with the Warĩnga novel. And since it is no longer a secret, I also have spent parts of the daytime writing it. Scrap paper has proved to be not as plentiful as I had been led to believe. Or the guard in charge is proving to be mean. Other political prisoners have been generous. Mathenge has given me all his reserve of paper; others have chipped in with the little they have.

But tonight I am back to writing on toilet paper. Of course there have been a few signs of some movement. We have been allowed to buy books through the warder in charge of the block. As a test case, Gĩkonyo places an order for *Petals of Blood*, and I for copies of Wole Soyinka's *The Man Died* and Meja Mwangi's *Going Down River Road*. *Petals of Blood* has been bought and brought to us, and has been read by all the political prisoners who can read English. Also *Going Down River Road*. But a paperback copy of *The Man Died* is not available. Within the same last two months, a new doctor has come and examined us all. The commissioner of prisons has also called once and acceded to our request for toothbrushes and toothpaste.

And today, this morning, December 11, 1978, the SSP agreed to virtually all our requests for sheets and a special diet from tomorrow, December 12. But nobody dares trust the signs of the times, no matter how potent, and the prevailing mood is one of gloom.

Warĩnga . . . Njoki . . . my symbols of hope and defiance.

I hear the clinking of a bunch of keys. My cell is next to the tiny exercise yard, so I always hear the noise of the main door into the block whenever it is being opened. Prison officers or corporals on night duty often make unexpected visits to see if the night guards are doing their watching properly.

Whenever I hear the clinking of keys and the noise of doors opening and closing, I normally wake up and tiptoe to the door. Through the barred opening in my door, I look at the faces and try to catch one or two words, all in an attempt to see if I can get news related to the world outside. I have never succeeded in getting any, but I keep on going through the ritual.

Tonight, however, I just sit at my desk. To hell with the ritual! I don't care if the prison officer or anybody catches me writing the novel on "their" rationed toilet paper. It's not my fault. I couldn't get enough of the scrap paper the SSP had promised. The novel is virtually complete and I am possessed. Imagination, once let loose, keeps on racing ahead, and the hand cannot keep pace with it.

Somebody is watching me through the window bars. I know it even before raising my head to meet the eyes of the new SSP. He lingers there as if he wants to speak to me. I walk to the door.

"Ngũgĩ, you are now free."

I am the first political prisoner to hear these words. I shout the news across the walls. "Free! . . . We are now free!"

I am no longer K6,77. I have regained my name, Ngũgĩ wa Thiong'o.

And when the door to cell 16 is finally open, the first thing I do is to rush to the compound to hug darkness (which I have not seen for a year) and look at the stars.

We are free. . . . We are free . . . and I feel certain that at home my mother, Wanjikũ, my wife, Nyambura, the children, and the good people of Limuru and Kenya are gazing at the same stars!

With me, going out of the Kamĩtĩ Maximum Security Prison, is my novel, *Caitaani Mũtharabainĩ* (*Devil on the Cross*), written on toilet paper.

Prison Break

Notes

1. Free Thoughts on Toilet Paper

1. Seven years of elementary schooling.

2. The novel has now appeared in Gĩkũyũ as *Caitaani Mũtharabainĩ* (East Africa Education Publishers, Nairobi, 1980), and the English translation appeared in 1981 under the title *Devil on the Cross.*

3. Christiaan Neethling Barnard, the South African surgeon who performed the world's first successful human-to-human heart transplant in 1967.

4. *I Will Marry When I Want.*

5. Leader of the Giriama people's resistance to British rule 1913–14. She was imprisoned and later exiled from her home area.

6. She was a healer and the intellect behind the Gusii warriors led by Otenyo, who fought the colonial forces led by Geoffry A. Northcote (whose name was pronounced Nyarigoti by the Gusii) in 1908. Otenyo was captured and beheaded, but Moraa continued urging resistance.

7. She led protests against the arrest of the workers' leader, Harry Thuku, in 1922. She and 150 others were massacred by the British colonial forces outside the central police station, the present site of the University of Nairobi.

8. Today I would probably call it global corporate capital (GCC).

9. From 1952 to 1960, thousands were herded into concentration camps.

10. It is difficult to find commonly accepted terms to best describe social class divisions in former colonies whose economy was and still is integrated into the Western imperialist economies. The word *comprador*, denoting a person or an economic class in a subordinate but mutually beneficial relationship with imperial corporate capital, as opposed to nationalistic capitalists, is still the most helpful term, particularly in the era of globalization.

11. "It's No Use," by Víctor-Jacinto Flecha. The translation, by Nick Caistor, appeared in *Index on Censorship*, vol. 8, no. 1 (London, Jan.–Feb. 1979).

12. They may have said Kīambu, but Tigoni was more likely, because they emphasized the short duration and the fewness of the questions.

13. Today there is a street in Nairobi, the capital city, named after Kīmathi. And in Uhuru Park, there is a monument, a memorial to all those who fought to liberate Kenya.

14. With the introduction of multiparty campaigns, followed by several largely "peaceful" elections and changes in leadership, the culture of fear and silence that I talk about is no longer as dominant. The democratic space has widened. But the old adage is still true: The price of liberty is eternal vigilance.

15. Pio Gama Pinto was the first Kenyan politician to be assassinated after independence, on February 24, 1965.

16. Assassinated on March 2, 1975.

17. See note 10 above.

18. When eventually I left prison, I learned that actually he was a friend of Reverend John Gatū, who indeed had been to see him and had asked him to check on my health. In my haste to judge and condemn, I even missed out on his hints as to whether I wanted him to carry greetings to my friends. Ideological purity blinded me, kept me from seeing that in opposites there are also possibilities that can

contribute to a positive. Did I expect him to join me in denouncing the government? Or his religion?

2. Parasites in Paradise

1. The Happy Valley has long fascinated writers, and many books have been written about it. The one that comes closest to the conception of the one I had signed the contract to write in 1967 is *White Mischief* (1982) by James Fox. It was turned into a film of the same title, directed by Michael Radford, in 1987.

2. She died in 1987.

3. In 2005, the current heir to the Delamere family estate, Thomas Cholmondeley, shot dead an African, was not imprisoned for it, and within the same year, shot dead another one. For the second shooting, he was detained until trial for several years, and then when prosecuted, he got a sentence reduced for time served.

4. On December 31, 1980 the Norfolk Hotel was bombed by unknown persons, but the Lord Delamere bar remained intact.

5. In my third memoir, *Birth of a Dream Weaver*, I have revisited this story because of how the "will to die" theory of the African came to play a big role in legal justification for massacres during the years of the State of Emergency, 1952–1960.

3. Colonial Lazarus Rises from the Dead

1. In their book *Public Law and Political Change in Kenya*, Y.P. Ghai and J.P.W.B. MacAuslan have detailed evidence and comment on the colonial basis of independent Kenya's laws—including the detention laws, regulations, and rules—and on their purpose: "to be a tool at the disposal of the dominant political and economic groups."

2. Scouts or spies.

3. After the fall of the Moi dictatorship, detention without trial was repealed in the new constitution that governs Kenya today.

4. The Culture of Silence and Fear

1. The Iregi was a generation of revolutionary rebels who had overthrown the corrupt dictatorial regime of "King" Gĩkũyũ and established ruling councils and procedures for handing over power, an event commemorated in the Ituĩka festival. The last such festival was held toward the end of the nineteenth century. The next, due in about 1930, was banned by the colonial overlords as a threat to public peace and order. See Jomo Kenyatta, *Facing Mount Kenya*.

2. A little reminiscent of the Chilean Victor Lidio Jara, who, after the American-engineered anti-Allende coup of September 11, 1973, was arrested, interrogated, and tortured by Pinochet but even while dying tried to reach for his guitar to sing one more song of love, peace, and social justice.

3. I was once a beneficiary of Richard Frost. I never met him, but he enabled my British Council Scholarship for postgraduate studies at Leeds University. I have touched on the contradictory impact of the British Council on my literary and intellectual formation in my other memoir, *Birth of a Dream Weaver*.

4. A trans-Africa highway has now been built through Kamĩrĩthũ and has drained the defiant pool.

5. See *Dreams in a Time of War*.

6. See *In the House of the Interpreter*.

7. Later he would become an MP for Limuru.

5. Wrestling with Colonial Demons

1. Harry Thuku, through his assistant, Desai, was in touch with the Gandhi movement in India and the Marcus Garvey movement in the United States. Recently I have argued that it was the danger he posed as a possible link between the two movements that really prompted his arrest and imprisonment without trial.

2. This and most subsequent extracts from speeches by Jomo Kenyatta are taken from Jeremy Murray-Brown's *Kenyatta* (New York: Dutton, 1973).

3. In his book *Revolution and Counter-Revolution in Germany*, Engels has aptly described the social basis of the vacillating character and psychology of the petit bourgeoisie:

> Its intermediate position between the class of larger capitalists, traders, manufacturers, the bourgeoisie proper so-called, and the proletarian or industrial class, determines its character. Aspiring to the position of the first, the least adverse turn of fortune hurls the individuals of this class down into the ranks of the second. . . . Thus eternally tossed about between the hope of entering the ranks of the wealthier class, and the fear of being reduced to the state of proletarians or even paupers; between the hope of promoting their interests by conquering a share in the direction of public affairs, and the dread of rousing, by ill-timed opposition, the ire of a government which disposes of their very existence, because it has the power of removing their best customers; possessed of small means, the insecurity of the possession of which is in the inverse of the amount—this class is extremely vacillating in its views.

4. In my memoirs, *Dreams in a Time of War* and *In the House of the Interpreter,* I have painted a more sympathetic image of Mbiyū Koinange, because of his concept of self-reliance, with its roots to his time at Virginia's Hampton Institute, the alma mater of Booker T. Washington. Probably inspired by Tuskegee Institute, he became the mind behind the construction of Gĩthũngũri Teachers College, on a self-help basis. Gĩthũngũri was the first college of higher education in Kenya but was banned in 1952. A symbol of people's self reliance, Gĩthũngũri was turned into a prison where captured soldiers of the Kenya Land and Freedom Army were hanged. A symbol of pride was turned into one of humiliation and defeat.

5. See chapter 3.

6. There are the well-known Pio Gama Pinto, assassinated after independence, and Fritz D'Souza, once speaker of the House after independence.

7. Meditations!

1. Ngong, or Ngong Hills, the site of Josiah Mwangi Kariũki's torture and death, had become a metaphor for state-induced disappearances of opponents of the governing regime.

2. There was a period during Idi Amin's military dictatorship in Uganda when the regime lost all control over the export of coffee from Uganda. Chepkube, on the border between Kenya and Uganda, became the center for coffee smuggled from Uganda. The Kenyan middlemen would get it very cheaply, then make a killing at the regular market.

3. For more on the conference, see my third memoir, *Birth of a Dream Weaver*.

4. Kofi Awoonor, after decades of distinguished service always guided by his pan-African consciousness, would eventually meet a tragic end as one of the victims of the al-Shabaab Islamist massacre at the Westgate shopping mall in Nairobi. It is the tragedy of postcolonial African politics that such a committed pan-Africanist would die a victim of *African* terrorists. Imperialism always gains when its victims are divided on ethnic and religious lines. A disunited Africa only helps Western imperialism and the enemies of African progress.

8. Dreams of Freedom

1. On looking back, I realize I was too harsh. Kenyatta's life, October 20, 1891–August 22, 1978, spanned the entire history of Kenya, precolonial, colonial, and postcolonial. He embodied that history and all its contradictions. Remarkably, from the 1920s to 1963, he remained the symbolic head of the anticolonial resistance, and nothing can take away from the fact he led us into independence.

About the Author

One of the leading African writers and scholars at work today, **Ngũgĩ wa Thiong'o** was born in Limuru, Kenya, in 1938. He is the author of *Wizard of the Crow*; *A Grain of Wheat*; *Weep Not, Child*; *Petals of Blood*; and *Birth of a Dream Weaver* (The New Press). He is currently Distinguished Professor of English and Comparative Literature at the University of California, Irvine.

Publishing in the
Public Interest

Thank you for reading this book published by The New Press. The New Press is a nonprofit, public interest publisher. New Press books and authors play a crucial role in sparking conversations about the key political and social issues of our day.

We hope you enjoyed this book and that you will stay in touch with The New Press. Here are a few ways to stay up to date with our books, events, and the issues we cover:

- Sign up at www.thenewpress.com/subscribe to receive updates on New Press authors and issues and to be notified about local events
- Like us on Facebook: www.facebook.com/new pressbooks
- Follow us on Twitter: www.twitter.com/thenew press

Please consider buying New Press books for yourself; for friends and family; and to donate to schools, libraries, community centers, prison libraries, and other organizations involved with the issues our authors write about.

The New Press is a 501(c)(3) nonprofit organization. You can also support our work with a tax-deductible gift by visiting www.thenewpress.com/donate.